BEIJING
ENCOUNTER

EILÍS QUINN

Beijing Encounter

Published by Lonely Planet Publications Pty Ltd
ABN 36 005 607 983

Australia	Head Office, Locked Bag 1, Footscray, Vic 3011
	☎ 03 8379 8000 fax 03 8379 8111
	talk2us@lonelyplanet.com.au
USA	150 Linden St, Oakland, CA 94607
	☎ 510 893 8555
	toll free 800 275 8555
	fax 510 893 8572
	info@lonelyplanet.com
UK	2nd Fl, 186 City Rd, London ECV1 2NT
	☎ 020 7106 2100 fax 020 7106 2101
	go@lonelyplanet.co.uk

This title was commissioned in Lonely Planet's Melbourne office and produced by: **Commissioning Editors** Rebecca Chau, George Dunford **Coordinating Editors** Monique Choy, Simon Williamson **Coordinating Cartographer** Joshua Geoghegan **Layout Designer** Cara Smith **Senior Editor** Sasha Baskett **Managing Cartographer** David Connolly **Cover Designer** Nic Lehman **Project Manager** Chris Love **Series Designers** Nic Lehman, Wendy Wright **Managing Layout Designers** Adam McCrow, Celia Wood **Thanks to** Quentin Frayne, Laura Jane, Yuanfang Ji, Yvonne Kirk, Lisa Knights, Rebecca Lalor

Cover photograph Bicycle and pedestrians on Tiananmen Square in front of the Forbidden Palace, Peter Solness/LPI. **Internal photographs** All photographs by Lonely Planet Images, and by Greg Elms except p114 by Krzyztof Dydynski; p128 Richard l'Anson; p27 Ray Laskowitz; p132 Keren Su; p30, p30, p135 Phil Weymouth; p25 Lawrie Williams.

All images are copyright of the photographers unless otherwise indicated. Many of the images in this guide are available for licensing from **Lonely Planet Images:** www.lonelyplanetimages.com.

ISBN 978 1 74104 666 3

Printed through Colorcraft Ltd, Hong Kong.
Printed in China.

HOW TO USE THIS BOOK
Colour-Coding & Maps

Colour-coding is used for symbols on maps and in the text that they relate to (eg all eating venues on the maps and in the text are given a green fork symbol). Each neighbourhood also gets its own colour, and this is used down the edge of the page and throughout that neighbourhood section.

Shaded yellow areas on the maps denote 'areas of interest' – for their historical significance, their attractive architecture or their great bars and restaurants. We encourage you to head to these areas and just start exploring!

Send us your feedback We love to hear from readers — your comments help make our books better. We read every word you send us, and we always guarantee that your feedback goes straight to the appropriate authors. The most useful submissions are rewarded with a free book. To send us your updates and find out about Lonely Planet events, newsletters and travel news visit our award-winning website: *www.lonelyplanet.com/contact*.

Note: We may edit, reproduce and incorporate your comments in Lonely Planet products such as guidebooks, websites and digital products, so let us know if you don't want your comments reproduced or your name acknowledged. For a copy of our privacy policy visit *www.lonelyplanet.com/privacy*.

EILÍS QUINN

Eilís grew up in Vancouver, Canada, where visits to the city's massive Chinatown sowed a fascination with China and foreign languages. A degree in East Asian Studies finally took her to the Middle Kingdom for real, where she fell for Beijing's manic energy the moment she got off the plane. Back in Canada, with degrees in Chinese, Russian and German, she resisted the pull of yet another language degree and opted for journalism instead, going on to work in newsrooms in the United States and Canada. She has previously authored Lonely Planet's *Best of Beijing* and contributed to the *China* and *China's Southwest* guides.

EILÍS' THANKS

Many thanks to the gang in Beijing especially Claire (I would have never made it to the airport without you), Mr Liu from Haidian (for saving the day with a smile when he certainly didn't have to) and Scarlett and Patrick, for such incredible hospitality. A huge thank you is also due to all the travellers who helped me out with their tips and time, you've all made this a better book.

THE PHOTOGRAPHER

Greg Elms has been a contributor to Lonely Planet for over 15 years. Armed with a Bachelor of Arts in Photography, Greg was a photographer's assistant for two years before embarking on a travel odyssey. He eventually settled down to a freelance career in Melbourne, and now works regularly for magazines, graphic designers, advertising agencies and, of course, book publishers such as Lonely Planet.

Our readers Many thanks to the travellers who wrote to us with helpful hints, useful advice and interesting anecdotes. Yvonne & Brendan Colley, Dorothy Hayes, Alfonso Arias Hormaechea, Barny Lucas, Kevin O'Connor, Matthew Overland, Annelies Ras, Chloe See and Keith Wilkinson.

Loads of characters crowd Wangfujing Snack Street (p49)

CONTENTS

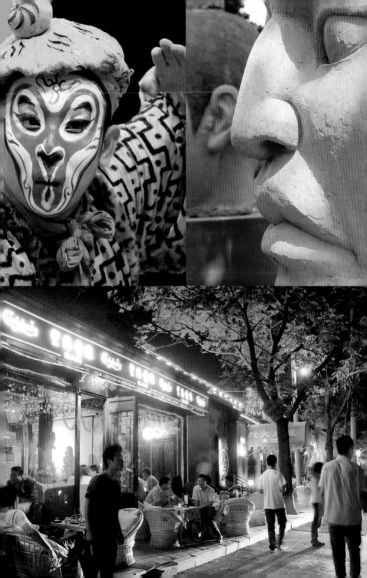

THIS IS BEIJING

Capital of China, host of the 2008 Olympics and home to one-of-a-kind dynastic wonders, Beijing is among the 21st century's most thrilling places to be.

It's a city with stunning historical sights, an outstanding collection of active temples and pockets of traditional architecture straight out of a story book. But Beijing also has sizzling nightlife and one of the most exciting contemporary art scenes in East Asia. It's also home to thousands of restaurants, representing all of China's provincial cuisines – for many, a gastronomic tour of the city would be reason enough to come.

As if all that wasn't enough, Beijingers themselves have long been the city's best-kept secret. They're brash and outspoken (in a city of 15 million one hardly has a choice to be otherwise) but this is tempered with a refreshing in-your-face curiosity and wickedly good sense of humour. The awarding of the Summer Games to the capital has created a palpable confidence and swagger in the population and locals are becoming less wary of foreigners. Everyone from business moguls to street sweepers goes out of their way to make visitors welcome these days.

But it's also a noisy and chaotic time for Beijing. The goodies bestowed on the city in the run-up to the Summer Games are unparalleled as the capital transforms from a stodgy Asian capital to an international city. New roads are being thrown down and skyscrapers built up seemingly overnight. Beijing is as likely to make the news these days for its latest daring architectural commission as it is for its out-of-control pollution. The rate of change (both societal and economic) excites, confuses and frustrates the local population in equal measure.

It all means that there's probably no more fascinating place to be at the moment. A ticket to Beijing doesn't just guarantee you a fabulous trip, it gets you a front row seat to the biggest story in the world.

Top left A Peking Opera performance (p20) at Chaoyang Theatre **Top right** The high-profile Dashanzi Art District (p16) **Bottom** Neon and nightlife – Houhai Lake (p120) offers plenty of both

>HIGHLIGHTS

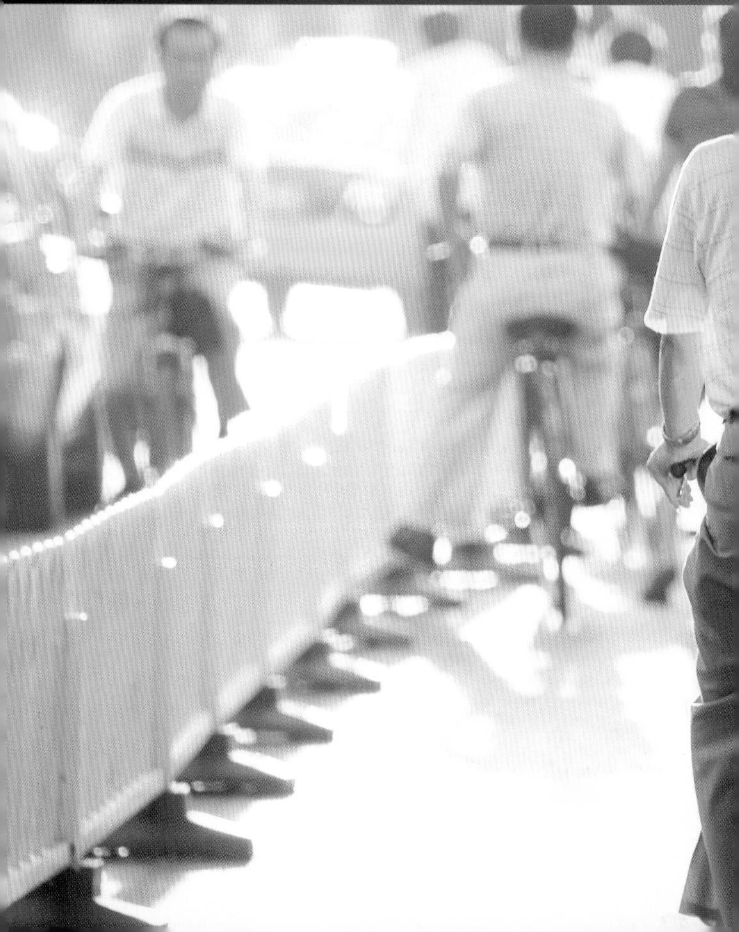

Join locals on the Tour de Beijing (p129)

HIGHLIGHTS

>1 FORBIDDEN CITY 故宮

WALK IN ROYALTY'S FOOTSTEPS AT THE FORBIDDEN CITY

The Forbidden City, home to 24 different Chinese emperors, is the best-preserved collection of ancient architecture in China and was the stage for five centuries of royal intrigue, drama and scandal.

The palace was originally established by Emperor Yongle (via a million labourers) between 1406 and 1420. With 800 buildings covering 720,000 sq metres, the palace is so large that a full-time restoration squad is continuously repainting and repairing. It's estimated to take 10 years to do a full renovation.

The buildings you see today are mainly post-18th century. Fire has always been a threat to the wooden palace, with six major, and countless minor, blazes sending buildings up in smoke. Many fires were the result of fireworks displays gone awry or wayward lanterns. Invading Manchus burned the palace to the ground in 1644 and eunuchs torched a number of buildings in 1923 in an attempt to cover up their looting of palace treasures. Imperial guards fought the blazes with water stored in huge vats, many of which still dot the palace grounds.

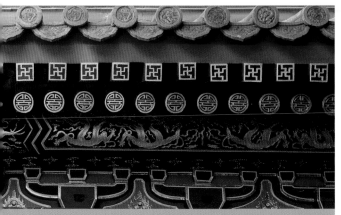

Fourteen Ming emperors and 10 Qing emperors called the Forbidden City home. Many became absorbed in the splendour of life inside the palace. The royal mealtime took up much of the day. By the time Empress Cixi took power she was getting twice-daily meals consisting of over 100 dishes. Prepared by an army of 450 kitchen workers, each had to be deemed nutritious and pleasing to the eye.

This lap of luxury could be a detriment to imperial rule and Chinese leaders were often ignorant of the living conditions outside the palace walls. Often emperors would hand over the dull task of ruling to the court eunuchs in order to take up the more interesting hobbies of collecting concubines or writing poetry.

Though most people think of the Forbidden City as a vast collection of buildings, it is actually a huge museum with the largest collection of imperial artefacts in the country, including a spectacular Ming dynasty–era crown bedecked with almost every precious metal and gemstone imaginable. The Forbidden City holdings are so large only a fraction of the collection can be shown at any one time.

These exhibits are scattered throughout the grounds, usually in the halls formerly used as the concubines' or eunuchs' living quarters. For more information, see p44.

>2 TIANANMEN SQUARE 天安门广场

DODGE KITES ON THE WORLD'S BIGGEST URBAN SQUARE

As the world's largest public square, Tiananmen Square is just as vast and awe-inspiring as you may have imagined. Most visitors end up criss-crossing this 440,000 sq metre plaza several times as they make their way between the Forbidden City (p11), Qianmen (p43), the Chairman Mao Memorial Hall (p39) and the Great Hall of the People (p42). Night-time here is especially beautiful when the tour groups thin out and hundreds of locals arrive to unfurl high-altitude, glow-in-the-dark kites.

The square is named for Tiananmen Gate (Gate of Heavenly Peace, p43), an arched 15th-century gate that lies just north of the square. Chinese royalty and communist leaders alike have used Tiananmen, restored in the 17th century, as a rostrum for viewing troops and for proclaiming the law of the land to assembled crowds.

Seven parallel bridges lead over a stream from the square to the gate's five doors. In imperial days the centre bridge and door could only be used by the emperor. Since the arrival of the communists, this door has been crowned with an enormous portrait of Mao. To the helmsman's left is written 'Long Live the People's Republic of China' and to his right, 'Long Live the Unity of the Peoples of the World'.

For many people, Tiananmen Square is irrevocably twinned with some of China's defining historical moments. Mao proclaimed the People's Republic of China from atop Tiananmen Gate on 1 October 1949 as Beijingers cheered in the plaza below. Later, the square was the sight of the 1989 pro-democracy student demonstrations that came to an end when government tanks rolled onto Beijing's side streets.

TIANANMEN FLAG CEREMONY

Tiananmen Square's flag is lowered every evening at sunset. The soldiers are drilled to march at 108 paces per minute, 75cm per pace. It's so precisely timed, the flag disappears underneath Tiananmen Gate at exactly the same second that the sun disappears. The same thing happens in reverse at sunrise except with a scratchy recording of the Chinese national anthem playing in the background.

Ever since, the square has been closely monitored by security cameras, People's Liberation Army (PLA) soldiers, and plain-clothes agents ready to pounce at the first sign of trouble. Despite children running wild and tourists snapping photos, the atmosphere at the square remains so reverent, it may be the only place in Beijing where you see people respect the 'no spitting' signs.

>3 SUMMER PALACE 圆明园

ESCAPE THE HEAT AND DECAMP TO THE ROYALS' SUMMER PLAYGROUND

Built in the 18th century, this is where the royal court came to escape the Beijing summer heat (apparently just as unbearable then as it is now). Though it's the Forbidden City that conjures up images of imperial power for most people, many historians believe the Summer Palace often functioned as the official royal residence and that the imperial court often stayed for more than half the year.

But despite the name, the Summer Palace isn't really a palace at all. Rather, it's a stunning complex of pavilions and temples built along the grounds surrounding Kunming Lake. Everything the royals could want or need was built here, including a theatre for Peking opera and temples on Longevity Hill featuring everything from Chinese Confucian symbols to Tibetan Buddhist features.

Though the area had long been the site of royal gardens, it was Emperor Qianlong (1711–99) who turned it into the Summer Palace we know today. One-hundred-thousand labourers were drafted for the job, which included landscaping as well as deepening and widening Kunming Lake.

The Summer Palace was off-limits to foreigners for much of the Qing dynasty. When Anglo-French troops finally stormed the compound during the Second Opium War and saw it for real they are said to have been so awed by what they saw that they forgot their orders.

Foreign troops stormed in again after defeating the Boxer rebels in 1900 and many of the Summer Palace's treasures were pillaged. Though some repairs were done, major restoration work didn't get going again until 1949.

See p83 for more information.

WALKING THE WESTERN CORRIDOR

The Western Corridor (see Map p83) is possibly the most beautiful part of the Summer Palace. An artificial spit of land, it's as narrow as 4m in many places, connected with precariously arched stone bridges and lined on both sides by weeping willow trees. This is where locals hang out when they visit, and no matter how many tour groups flood the Summer Palace's imperial residences or temples, walking the western corridor will give you a peaceful and unique peek into a little-visited part of the palace.

>4 FACTORY 798/DASHANZI ART DISTRICT 大山子艺术区

SNAP UP CONTEMPORARY ART'S NEXT BIG THING AT FACTORY 798

China's red-hot art market gets almost as much press as the Olympics do and there's no better place to buy into it than here. This gutted factory houses over 100 galleries and artist studios, turning the area into a creative hub.

The factory halls were built in the 1950s with Soviet Union money and East German architectural and industrial know-how. It went on to churn out electronics for decades before being shut down as Beijing urbanised and its industrial sector moved further away from the city centre. In 2002 the city's artistic community started to take an interest in this giant industrial carcass, moving in and making it the city's artistic hotbed.

Cash-flush Beijing entrepreneurs have recently started investing their extra cash in local artists, sending prices through the roof. An original Yue Minjun at US$100,000 a pop may be out of your reach, but there are hundreds of emerging artists waiting to be discovered.

If you're new to the art scene, buy pieces because you love them, not for their investment potential (many believe the Chinese art market is due for a downturn). The owner of a gallery you particularly like can also make suggestions, but remember, the only guiding rule should be whether you like it or not. See also p56.

>5 MODERN ARCHITECTURE
KEEP UP WITH BEIJING'S CHANGING SKYLINE

How things have changed. Ten years ago, it was rare to find 'Beijing' and 'modern architecture' in the same sentence. But these days, new additions to the skyline are making headline news, not just in China but all over the world.

The Bird's Nest (National Stadium, p103), by Swiss architectural firm Herzog & de Meuron, and the Water Cube (National Aquatics Centre, p103), by Australian firm PTW Architects, have got the lion's share of the attention. Most Beijingers see the buildings as culturally relevant (bird's nest is a Chinese culinary delicacy and the Water Cube is seen as appropriate 'yin' to the stadium's 'yang') and consider them powerful symbols of modern Beijing. The new Cui Kai–designed Capital Museum (p88) as well as the Commune at the Great Wall (see the boxed text, p107) are also well liked.

Other buildings are more controversial. Many locals find the new CCTV Headquarters (p74), the brainchild of Dutch designers Rem Koolhaas and Ole Scheeren, objectively impressive but not 'Chinese enough' for downtown Beijing.

And nothing gets a Beijinger on a rant faster than asking their opinion of the new National Grand Theatre (p92), designed by French architect Paul Andreu. Despite some remarkable features, including a moat, a see-through shell and underwater entrances, many locals complain the theatre is little more than a giant egg, a disrespectful form to build so close to the Forbidden City.

>6 TEMPLE OF HEAVEN 天坛公园

EXPLORE MING ARCHITECTURE AT THE CITY'S MOST POPULAR TEMPLE

No matter how much you've travelled, you've probably never seen a temple quite like this one. With enough symbolism and numerology to boggle the mind, the Ming architecture here is unforgettable.

As a major place of ritual worship for Chinese royalty, everything about this complex is built for the view of the gods. Seen from above, the temples are round and their bases square, a pattern chosen to reflect the ancient Chinese belief that heaven is round and earth is square. The shape of the 273-hectare park also reflects this, with the northern end a semicircle and the southern end a square.

The Hall of Prayer for Good Harvests, mounted on a three-tiered marble terrace, is the temple's star attraction. The hall's ornate roof is also three-tiered and is decorated in stunning blue, yellow and green glazed tiles, representing heaven, earth and the mortal world. Inside the hall, immense pillars symbolise the four seasons and the 12 months of the year. Though a lightning-strike burnt the structure to a crisp in 1889, it was rebuilt the next year with fir trees shipped from Oregon. Thanks to ancient building methods, the whole structure (amazingly) sticks together without nails or cement.

South of here, the octagonal Imperial Vault (shaped like a mini-version of the Hall of Prayer for Good Harvests) held tablets belonging to the emperor's ancestors to be used during the winter solstice ceremony. The vault is surrounded by a stone fortification known as the Echo Wall. It's said to be such a perfect semicircle that a whisper at one end can be carried around to the other side. The Triple Sounds Stones lead up to the vault, so stand here, clap your hands and the echo should come back once from the first stone, twice from the second and thrice from the third. Visitors get a major kick out of these two 'interactive' spots, though it's hard to test out the claims for sure given that dozens of other people will be right next to you trying to do exactly the same thing.

Further south, the Round Altar is where the Emperor performed his rituals. It's a place of such importance that everything from the

marble stones to the columns and stairs are arranged in groups of nine or multiples of nine, a number considered 'imperial'.

When you visit, don't forget to check out the park's remoter areas. The Divine Music Administration (in the west side of the park) was used by the Japanese during WWII as a bacterial laboratory but now houses a collection of traditional Chinese instruments. English captions explain their use during imperial ceremonies and there are demonstrations roughly once an hour during the summer. See also p69.

>7 PEKING OPERA 京剧

GET A FRONT-ROW SEAT AT BEIJING'S OLDEST ART FORM

Love it or hate it, you'll never forget your first Peking opera performance. With a madcap mix of piercing song, elaborate costumes and frantic acrobats, it may take some getting used to but it's absolutely worth the effort.

Over 900 years old, Peking opera is China's most famous form of theatre incorporating martial arts, poetic arias and stylised dance. Traditionally, only men could be performers and they were at the very bottom of the social ladder, on a par with prostitutes and slaves. Despite this, opera remained a popular form of entertainment, included in festivals, marriages and even funerals.

Most performances were open-air, compelling performers to develop a piercing style of singing that could be heard above the crowds, and to wear garish costumes that could be seen through the poor lighting of oil lamps. Performances continue to be loud and bright, with singers taking on stylised roles instantly recognised by Peking opera fans. The four major roles are the female role, the male role, the 'painted-face' role (for gods and warriors) and the clown. There's an excellent choice of places to watch Peking opera in Beijing including the Huguang Guild Hall (p99) and the Lao She Teahouse (p99). To learn more, the Mei Lanfang Former Residence (p89) has costumes and sometimes terrific temporary exhibits on understanding the art form. If you'd prefer to see some acrobatics, see p128.

>8 PEKING DUCK 北京烤鸭

GORGE YOURSELF ON BEIJING'S SIGNATURE DISH

Tucking into Beijing's trademark dish is as much a part of visiting the city as taking in Tiananmen Square. Once an imperial delicacy, it's said that Peking duck went mainstream after the fall of the Qing dynasty and scores of royal chefs were out of work. Many opened restaurants and the public quickly fell in love with the special duck recipe.

It's not an easy dish to master, however. First, the duck is inflated by blowing air between its skin and body. The skin is then pricked and the duck is doused in boiling water. Finally, it's hung up to air dry before being roasted. When cooked, the duck's skin is crispy on the outside and juicy on the inside. It's then cut up and served with sauce, pancakes, green onions and cucumber.

These days, every restaurant has a different version of the recipe, and Beijingers can discuss the merits and faults of each version for hours. See p122 for a list of some popular restaurants.

>9 PANJIAYUAN ANTIQUE MARKET
潘家园古玩市场

HIT BEIJING'S MOST FAMOUS FLEA MARKET BEFORE DAWN

Every weekend, over 3000 sellers and tens of thousands of shoppers flood Panjiayuan for the most thrilling shopping spectacle in Beijing. Get here before sunrise, however, and it will be just you, the merchants and dozens of flashlight-wielding antique aficionados. Watching these collectors scour the aisles for that Ming vase nobody's noticed or the Qing-era sculpture that somehow survived both war and the Cultural Revolution is a sight in itself. The haggling can be so skilled and nuanced, onlookers have been known to applaud with approval.

The Panjiayuan Market started in the early 1990s, slowly making a name for itself after several well-publicised finds by amateur collectors. The market has grown in space and reputation ever since.

These days, however, the chances of regular folks stumbling across a priceless treasure are pretty remote. The antique hobbyists and dealers line up on Saturday for the 4.30am opening and have usually scooped up everything of possible value long before the general public has even gotten out of bed. But no matter, the range and variety of goods makes Panjiayuan a must-see and one of the most colourful and exciting spots in Beijing. See p75.

>10 HUTONG 胡同

GET LOST IN THE CITY'S TRADITIONAL ALLEYWAYS

Strolling the capital's mazelike *hutong* (alleyways) is a rare window into traditional Beijing and a unique and exciting way to experience the city. These alleyways teem with life and are intensely social. Everywhere you look, people are sitting outside, taking their songbirds for walks or getting together an open-air mah jong game.

As the city modernises, these lanes are being gobbled up by construction crews faster than people can keep track. For the moment, however, several fascinating pockets remain. Xuanwu (p94), Chongwen (p66), Dongcheng (p38) and Xicheng (p86) are all good areas to explore.

The government, recognising the tourism potential, has pledged to preserve several of these old neighbourhoods, proclaiming 25 so-called 'protected *hutong* areas' in central Beijing. Though people are hopeful, many doubt this policy will last for long.

For visitors, it's best to dive in while you can. If you don't want to do it solo, rickshaw-driver tours are plentiful around Qianhai Lake (Map p87, D3) and the Drum and Bell Towers (Map pp40–1, B3). Don't worry about finding the drivers, they'll find you. The China Culture Club (p154) also offers excellent tours.

>11 CITY PARKS 公园

EXCERCISE YOUR *QI* AMONG THE LOCALS AT A CITY PARK

Beijing's city parks aren't just green spaces, they're the city's social hubs. With most Beijingers crammed into communal housing for the last 50 years, the neighbourhood park has become everyone's big backyard. Parks are where Beijingers go to stretch their legs, play musical instruments, practise their singing or walk their songbirds. It's where they meet with hundreds of their closest friends to practise martial arts or the Viennese waltz. Temple of Heaven Park (p69) is the best place to see taichi (and get asked to join in). Jingshan Park (p42) is popular with dancers on weekends practising everything from the foxtrot to traditional Chinese fan routines. Beihai Park (p88) is a magnet for water calligraphers as well as singers who like to practise their Peking opera arias at the park's Five Dragon Pavilion.

>BEIJING DIARY

Beijing is at its best and most fun when it erupts in the colour and excitement of its traditional festivals. 'Real life' grinds to a halt during these times and Beijingers let loose in response. Meanwhile out-of-towners flood sights to capacity and hotels jack up their room rates in welcome. The dates of many traditional festivals are based on the lunar calendar, and so will take place at different times each year. But besides traditional celebrations, Beijing is increasingly hosting grassroots art and music festivals. Dates and locations can be notoriously loose, so bring a flexible attitude and double-check the websites before you arrive.

Burning incense in worship at Confucius Temple (p39)

JANUARY & FEBRUARY

Spring Festival

Also known as Chinese New Year, this is the mother of all Chinese holidays, when families flock together and firecrackers explode on every street corner. Everyone gets a week off and revellers camp out in front of TVs for variety-show marathons. It's usually late January/early February.

Lantern Festival

Fifteen days after the start of Spring Festival, lanterns go up in Beijing's major parks, marking the official end of Chinese New Year festivities as well as the first full moon of the New Year. Sweet rice dumplings (yuanxiao) are also eaten on this day.

MARCH, APRIL & MAY

Birth of Guanyin

Taking place on the 19th day of the second lunar month, this is the day to pay homage to the goddess Guanyin at Buddhist and Taoist temples around Beijing.

Tomb Sweeping Day

Chinese families tidy up their relatives' grave sites and burn paper money in honour of the deceased every 5 April (4 April in leap years).

International Labour Day

Held on 1 May, this day marks the beginning of a week-long holiday for just about everyone in the country. Many Chinese people use this break to hit the road, so

MUSIC & ART FESTIVALS TO KEEP AN EYE ON

Beijing Ninegates Jazz Festival (www.ninegate.com.cn) Music festival with local and international jazz acts over two weeks in May or June.

Midi Music Festival (www.midifestival.com in Chinese) Annual festival in May showcasing China's emerging underground bands.

Beijing Bienniale (www.namoc.org in Chinese) Held at Beijing's National Art Museum of China (p43) in odd-numbered years showcasing Chinese and international works.

Beijing Pop Festival (www.beijingpopfestival.com) Takes place every September in Chaoyang Park and hosts Chinese music heavyweights alongside international rap and rock acts. It's one of Asia's biggest outdoor shows.

Keep in mind that the Olympics and its related construction will be playing havoc with the dates and locations of lesser-known festivals in 2008 and 2009, so keep your ear to the ground when you arrive, and your eye on the local press (p154) for the latest on what's going on where.

The Lantern Festival – an illuminating event

tourist sights and transport are often choked to capacity.

JUNE, JULY & AUGUST

International Children's Day
Every 1 June is devoted to the kids, who celebrate by unfurling their kites till they block out the sky.

Anniversary of Founding of CCP
The founding of the Chinese Communist Party is celebrated on 1 July with plenty of enthusiastic flag waving on Tiananmen Square.

Anniversary of Founding of PLA
1 August brings you more official flag waving from Tiananmen Square to celebrate the founding of the People's Liberation Army.

Dragon Boat Festival
Held on the fifth day of the fifth lunar month (usually in June), dragon-boat races take place all over Beijing. The festival is a tribute to Qu Yuan, an honoured Chu official.

SEPTEMBER, OCTOBER & NOVEMBER

Mid-Autumn Festival

Held on the 15th or 18th day of the eighth lunar month (usually in September), this festival is also known as the Moon or Harvest Festival and is when families get together to eat moon cakes (*yuebing*; red-bean paste wrapped in pastry).

National Day

On 1 October, marching bands and soldiers are rolled out to commemorate the day Mao proclaimed the establishment of the People's Republic of China in his famous 1949 speech from Tiananmen Gate. The day is marked by over-the-top displays of military pageantry on Tiananmen Square.

Confucius' Birthday

The great philosopher's birthday is celebrated with a ceremony at Beijing's Confucius Temple (p39) on 27 October.

>ITINERARIES

Saturday night rush hour...on Houhai Lake (p120)

ITINERARIES

If you're short on time, it can be difficult to know where to start in a city the size of Beijing. Check out the itineraries below to help you tailor your trip. They'll give you ideas on how to fit in everything you want to experience in this madcap city.

DAY ONE

Wake up early and watch the flag raising ceremony on Tiananmen Square (p12). After buying breakfast from one of the street food vendors that will be circling you by now, be first in line when the Forbidden City (p44) opens at 8.30am and beat the tour-bus crowds. Take your time and check out the palace's far-flung areas and you may stumble upon one of its little-known historical exhibitions. Leave by the north exit and climb up the hill at Jingshan Park (p42) for unforgettable views of the palace rooftops. Then head down to Beihai Park's Fangshan Restaurant (p91) for a chance to eat like an emperor.

DAY TWO

Spend some time getting to know the contemporary side of Beijing. Start day two window-shopping along Wangfujing Dajie (Map pp40–1, C6) before taking the subway to Sanlitun Lu (Map pp54–5, D4) for lunch at one of its international restaurants such as Alameda (p59). When your appetite is sated, hop in a cab to the Factory 798/Dashanzi Art District (p56), where you can spend the afternoon browsing for contemporary art before ducking into a fashionable hangout such as Café Pause for a drink or the Jiang Hu Club for a leisurely meal.

DAY THREE

If day three falls on a Saturday or Sunday, head to the Panjiayuan Antique Market (p75) at dawn and try to outbid the antique dealers. If not, head up to Haidian District to roam around the Summer Palace (p83). Spend your time exploring the Qing-era buildings or doing a circuit around Kunming Lake, taking in the lovely Western Corridor. Come back by boat along the city's ancient canal network (p147) and

---

Top left White Cloud Temple (p89) covered in incense haze **Top right** A colour to suit any complexion at the Silk Market (p76) **Bottom** Rub shoulders with the beautiful people at World of Suzie Wong (p65)

maybe head to the Drum and Bell Towers (p42 and p39) to explore the *hutong* (alleyways), relax at one of the local bars like the Drum & Bell (p50) or check out a show at the controversial new National Grand Theatre (p92).

BLISSFUL BEIJING

If the cut and thrust of haggling has taken its toll or if navigating your way through the Forbidden City's crowds has left you drained, take a day out to recharge, Beijing-style. Roll out of bed at 6am to centre your *qi* (energy) alongside the crowds at the Temple of Heaven Park (p69). Then treat yourself to one of Beijing's famous foot massages at Bohdi (p64) or go to Beihai Park (p88) to practise the calming strokes of water calligraphy.

RAINY DAYS

When it rains in Beijing, it doesn't just pour, it comes down in buckets. The stellar Capital Museum (p88) is the best place to wait it out and has so many interactive exhibits you could while away the whole day here without even knowing. Rainy days are also the perfect time to hole up in one of Beijing's cosy family-style restaurants like Xiao Wang's (p77) or Xiangmanlou (p61).

FORWARD PLANNING

Three weeks before you go Book your hotel room right away, check whether your visit coincides with any major festivals (p25), start reading the *China Daily* (www.chinadaily .com.cn) weekend edition online for the big upcoming Beijing events and make sure your visa is in order. Buy a Chinese phrasebook.

One week before you go Research all the great expat resources (p154) for the latest in new nightclubs, interesting people in town, and the details on which stores and restaurants have been 'relocated' to make way for new construction. Rent *The Last Emperor* on DVD.

The day before you go Reconfirm your flight; print out the address of your hotel in Chinese to give to the taxi driver when you get to the airport; pack your Chinese phrasebook; and most importantly, make a dinner reservation at one of Beijing's most popular restaurants such as Liqun Roast Duck Restaurant (p71), the Courtyard (p48) or Green T House (p60).

FOR FREE

If you want to ease up on your wallet or purse, you won't be bored in Beijing. Though the city doesn't have the kind of 'free' or 'discount' museum days of some other cities, Beijing is so loaded with energy and activity there's enough street theatre to keep you entertained. Markets are particularly good spots, especially Dongjiao Shichang (p74) and the Panjiayuan Antique Market (p75). Ritan Park (p74) is one of Beijing's rare recreation spaces that doesn't charge an admission fee. Head to the former sun altar and see if anyone will let you join their kung-fu lesson for free.

>DISTRICTS

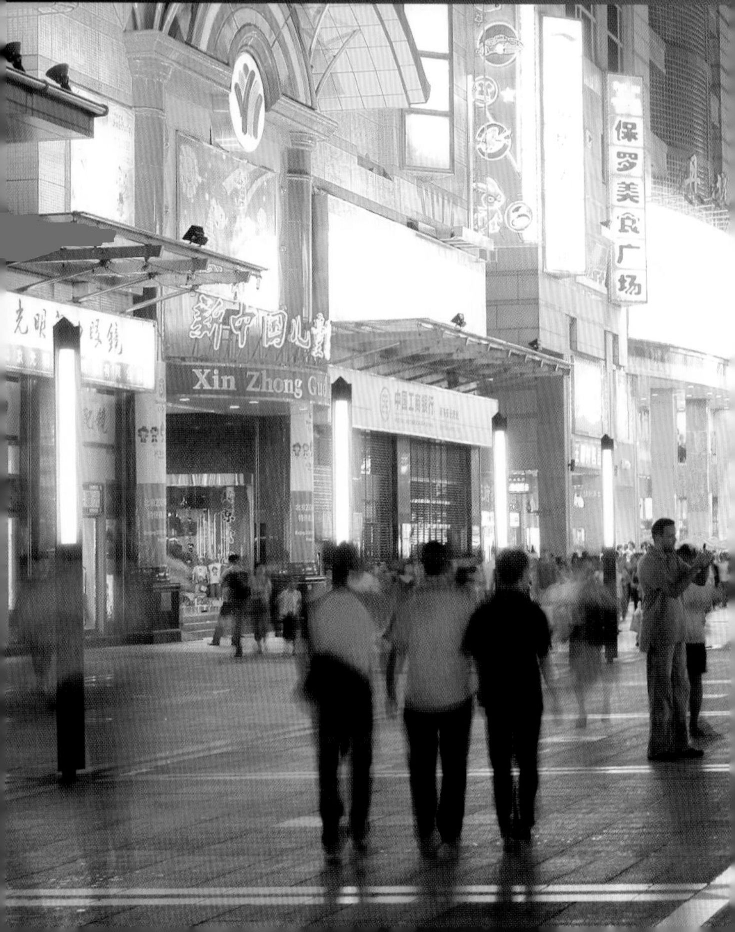

Pedestrians in Dashanzi Art District (p16)

DISTRICTS

Beijing's six main districts spiral out from the city's core and contain the very best of both the traditional and modern city.

Dongcheng lies at the heart of the city and contains many of Beijing's iconic sights such as Tiananmen Square and the former imperial palace. Nowadays it also gets plenty of buzz for its upscale shopping, fine dining and high-end accommodation. Next door, the districts of North and South Chaoyang swoop along the city's eastern flank, bracketing Dongcheng to the north and Chongwen to the south.

North Chaoyang is synonymous with wild nightlife. It has Beijing's most dynamic club and bar scene and draws drinkers and dancers from even the far-flung districts. Home to the city's embassies, it also has several of Beijing's best international restaurants. The Olympic Park, with its 'Bird's Nest' stadium and 'Water Cube' aquatics centre, lies in the district's north.

In South Chaoyang, there are great shopping areas and markets as well as the rapidly expanding Central Business District, where skyscrapers are being thrown up faster than people can count.

Southeast of the city centre, Chongwen has great Ming-era sights, including the spectacular Temple of Heaven and the lesser-known Ming City Wall Ruins Park and Southeast Watchtower. Neighbouring Xuanwu doesn't have as many formal sights but its traditional *hutong* (alleyways), speciality shopping streets and Peking opera venues make it unique in the city.

North of here, Xicheng (or 'West City') has some of Beijing's most daring new buildings including the Capital Museum. There's also a thriving nightlife and restaurant scene set up on the shores of Xicheng's Houhai Lake area.

Haidian looms northwest of central Beijing and has the city's best universities and most expansive parks and green spaces, as well as a vibrant student-driven bar scene.

Beijing's five-line subway system is still woefully inadequate given the city's vast size and 15-million strong population. Several new subway lines are planned and four are slated to open by June 2008.

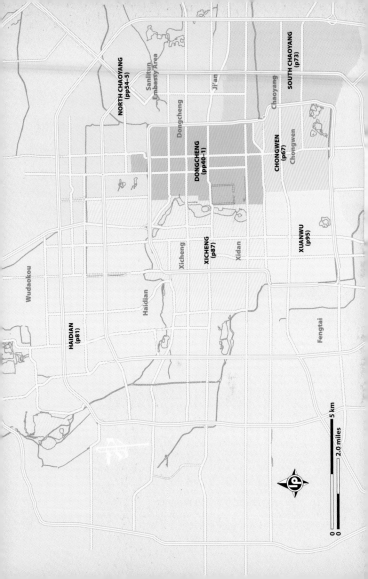

NORTH CHAOYANG (pp54–5)

Sanlitun
Embassy Area

Jian

SOUTH CHAOYANG (p73)

Dongcheng

Chaoyang

CHONGWEN (p67)

DONGCHENG (pp40–1)

Chongwen

Xicheng

XICHENG (p87)

Xidan

XUANWU (p95)

Haidian

Wudaokou

HAIDIAN (p81)

Fengtai

5 km

2.0 miles

0

0

DISTRICTS

DONGCHENG

>DONGCHENG 东城

With Tiananmen Square and the Forbidden City among other blockbuster sights, Dongcheng remains one of the most exciting districts in Beijing for visitors. Rising from its southern flank, Wangfujing Dajie is Dongcheng's main shopping artery. Most locals can't afford its designer malls and expensive department stores but the street still draws tens of thousands of people who window shop before heading to its famous snack streets for the city's best street food. In Dongcheng's north, the Drum and Bell Towers are the focal point of some lively *hutong* (alleyway) neighbourhoods. Some of Beijing's best new bars and restaurants recently opened in this area. The Lama Temple, a hub of Tibetan Buddhism, sits in the district's northeast.

By Beijing's standards, Dongcheng's subway network is pretty good, and it's improving. Line 5 recently opened, which means you can get from Dongcheng's southern Dongdan stop to Yonghegong-Lama Temple, in the district's north, in a matter of minutes.

DONGCHENG

Please see over for map

SEE

BEIJING IMPERIAL CITY ART MUSEUM 皇城艺术馆
☎ 8511 5114; 9 Changpu Heyan, 菖蒲河沿9号; adult/child Y20/10; ⏱ 10am-5.30pm, last entry 4.30pm; Ⓜ Tiananmen Dong
Visitor-friendly English captions (hurray!) bring this museum's permanent collection of fascinating Ming and Qing-era exhibits to life. Temporary exhibits include anything from modern Chinese art to imperial furniture.

BELL TOWER 钟楼
Zhonglouwan Hutong, 钟楼湾胡同; admission Y15; ⏱ 9am-5pm; Ⓜ Gulou Dajie
First constructed in 1272 but felled numerous times by fire and war, the tower's present structure dates from 1745. Climb up the steep steps (very carefully!) to gawk at the 63-tonne bell. The Drum Tower (p42) is just south.

CHAIRMAN MAO MEMORIAL HALL 毛主席纪念堂
☎ 6513 2277; Tiananmen Sq, 天安门广场; admission free; ⏱ 8.30-11.30am Tue-Sun, 2-4pm Tue & Thu, mornings only July & Aug; Ⓜ Qianmen
Mao's body has been pickled and put on display here since his death in 1976. Wackiness aside, Chinese visitors consider this serious business – snickering or eye-rolling isn't tolerated. The compulsory bag check (up to Y10 depending on size) is across the street. For more on Tiananmen Square, see p12.

CONFUCIUS TEMPLE & IMPERIAL COLLEGE 孔庙与国子监
☎ 8401 1977; 13 Guozijian Jie, 国子监街13号; admission Y10; ⏱ 9am-5pm, last entry 4pm; Ⓜ Yonghegong-Lama Temple
This is China's second-largest Confucius temple. Nearby, the Imperial College is where emperors spouted Confucian classics to rapt audiences. Shrouded in tarps and renovators at the time of research, the results should be on full display by the time you hit town.

Bell Tower – very appealing

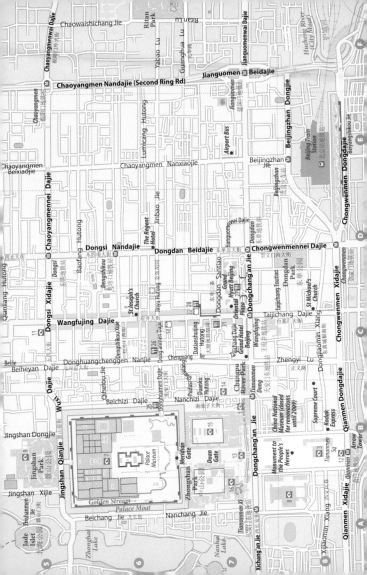

☉ DITAN PARK 地坛公园
☎ 6421 4657; Andingmen Dongdajie, 安定门东大街; admission Y2; ⏰ 6am-9.30pm; ⊕ Yonghegong-Lama Temple
Imperial rulers once made offerings to the Earth God from this park's square-shaped altar. Nowadays, local residents flood the park to gossip and power-walk along the shady lanes. An excellent temple fair takes place here during Spring Festival (see p26).

☉ DRUM TOWER 鼓楼
Gulou Dongdajie, 鼓楼东大街; admission Y20; ⏰ 9am-5pm; ⊕ Gulou Dajie
The ancient Chinese beat drums here to keep the minions punctual. Views from atop the tower are lovely and there's drumming demonstrations every half hour (9.10am to 11.30am and 1.30pm to 5pm, May to October). The Bell Tower (p39) is just to the north.

☉ GREAT HALL OF THE PEOPLE 人民大会堂
☎ 6309 6935; Tiananmen Sq, 天安门广场; adult/child 1 Apr-31 Oct Y20/5, 1 Nov-31 Mar Y10/5; ⏰ 8.30am-4.30pm 1 Apr-31 Oct, 9am-4.30pm 1 Nov-31 Mar, last entry 4pm; ⊕ Tiananmen Xi
Home of the National People's Congress, this intimidating Stalin-styled colossus is open to the public when Congress isn't sitting and the Chinese Communist Party

bigwigs aren't welcoming foreign heads of state. The compulsory bag check is Y2 to Y5. For details on Tiananmen Square, see p12.

☉ JINGSHAN PARK 景山公园
☎ 6403 8098; Jingshan Qianjie, 景山前街; admission Y2; ⏰ 6am-10pm; ⊕ Tiananmen Xi or Tiananmen Dong, then taxi
This park's hill, erected from earth excavated to construct the Forbidden City's moat, offers one of Beijing's most memorable views. Closer to the ground, dancing locals take to this park in droves, particularly the swing and ballroom set.

☉ LAMA TEMPLE 雍和宫
☎ 6404 4499; 12 Yonghegong Dajie, 雍和宫大街12号; admission Y35; ⏰ 9am-5pm, last entry 4.30pm; ⊕ Yonghegong-Lama Temple
Ornately decorated, this is one of Beijing's most spectacular places

of worship. Emperor Yongzheng lived here but ditched it for the Forbidden City in 1722, leaving the temple to Mongolian and Tibetan monks. Don't miss Wanfu Pavilion, the final hall, which contains an 18m-high statue of the Maitreya Buddha, reputedly sculpted from a single block of sandalwood. An audio guide is Y20, with a Y200 deposit.

◎ NATIONAL ART MUSEUM OF CHINA 中国美术馆
☎ 6401 7076; www.namoc.org in Chinese; 1 Wusi Dajie, 五四大街1号; adult/child/senior & student Y20/5/10; ◷ 9am-5pm Tue-Sun, last entry 4pm; ◎ Dongsi

This contemporary-art museum gets better and more professionally run each year. There's no permanent collection so you'll be in for an eclectic mix of Chinese and foreign art no matter when you come.

◎ QIANMEN 前门
☎ 6522 9384; Tiananmen Sq, 天安门广场; adult/child 1 Apr-31 Oct Y20/5, 1 Nov-31 Mar Y10/5; ◷ 8.30am-4.30pm 1 Apr-31 Oct, 9am-4.30pm 1 Nov-31 Mar, last entry 4pm; ◎ Qianmen

This 15th-century gate, also known as Zhengyangmen, was once part of the city wall that divided the ancient Inner City from the outside world. These

days, it contains excellent exhibits on Beijing city history. The Arrow Tower, just south of here, was also part of the ancient city wall but isn't open to the public. For details on Tiananmen Square, see p12.

◎ TIANANMEN GATE (GATE OF HEAVENLY PEACE) 天安门
Tiananmen Sq, 天安门广场; admission Y15; ◷ 8.30am-4.30pm; ◎ Tiananmen Xi or Tiananmen Dong

Climb up this massive gate, which is still adorned with its iconic Mao portrait, for a stunning bird's-eye view of Tiananmen Square (p12). The bag check (Y2 to Y6 depending on size) is compulsory.

◎ WAN FUNG ART GALLERY 云峰画廊
☎ 6523 3320; www.wanfung.com .cn; 136 Nanchizi Dajie, 南池子大街136号; ◷ noon-6pm Mon, 10am-6pm Tue-Sun; ◎ Tiananmen Dong

This Beijing branch of the Hong Kong–based gallery deals in contemporary Chinese figurative art in traditional mediums like oil or watercolour.

◎ WORKERS' CULTURAL PALACE 劳动人民文化宫
☎ 6525 2189; Dongchang'an Jie, 东长安街; admission Y2; ◷ 6am-9pm; ◎ Tiananmen Dong

The name's a turn-off but don't give this modest park a pass. It's

FORBIDDEN CITY 紫禁城

For 500 years commoners were prohibited from entering the **Forbidden City** (☎ 8511 7243; www.dpm.org.cn; Dongchang'an Jie, 天安门广场; admission Y60; ☽ 8.30am-5pm, last entry 4pm 16 Apr-15 Oct, 8.30am-4.30pm, last entry 3.30pm 16 Oct-15 Apr; ☻ Tiananmen Xi or Tiananmen Dong). Those who defied this ban, and entered uninvited, risked death. Fast-forward to the present day, however, and the Forbidden City welcomes countless visitors.

The Forbidden City was initially built (by as many as a million workers) under the auspices of Emperor Yongle between 1406 and 1420. For the next 500 years, until the revolution of 1911, this sprawling complex was the seat of Chinese government.

Despite its venerable age, the combination of wooden architecture and naked flame (lantern festivals, fireworks, arson) has meant that parts of the palace have been incinerated and rebuilt many times over the centuries. Consequently, much of the present-day Forbidden City dates from the 18th century onwards.

The city's vital statistics are mindboggling: 720,000 sq metres, 800 buildings, 9000 rooms. So vast is the complex that visitors could easily spend several days exploring its expanses. One possible itinerary is to start your explorations at the **Hall of Supreme Harmony**, the palace's biggest structure. This was the site of the imperial court's grandest events, including coronations and royal birthdays. Inside the hall, the throne is guarded by two *luduan*, mythical beasts who can understand all languages and cover a distance of 9000 leagues in a day.

North of here, the **Hall of Middle Harmony** was a kind of 'backstage' area where the emperor stopped to compose himself and consult with ministers before entering the Hall of Supreme Harmony. Next, the **Hall of Preserving Harmony** was first used for state banquets and later for imperial examinations. Behind the hall, a 17m marble carriageway carved with dragons leads up to the entrance.

The royals' former living quarters lie at the back of the palace grounds. The emperors' quarters were in the **Palace of Heavenly Purity**, which initially housed Ming and early Qing emperors, but later became an audience hall in which ambassadors and other luminaries were received. The empresses' quarters were in the **Palace of Earthly Tranquillity**.

Once palatial living quarters housing an assortment of libraries, temples, theatres and gardens, the western and eastern sides of the Forbidden City are now museums that require additional entry fees. Make sure you visit the **Imperial Treasure Gallery** (Y10), and don't miss the **Clocks & Watches Gallery** (admission Y10). The gallery boasts a dazzling array of timepieces, many of which were gifts to the Qing emperors from abroad.

At the northern end of the Forbidden City is the **Imperial Garden**, a classical Chinese garden with 7000 sq metres of fine landscaping, including rockeries, walkways, pavilions and ancient – carbuncular and deformed – cypresses.

An audio guide is available for Y40, with a Y100 deposit. Renovations on several of these buildings are ongoing, but all is expected to be wrapped up by spring 2008. For more background, see p11.

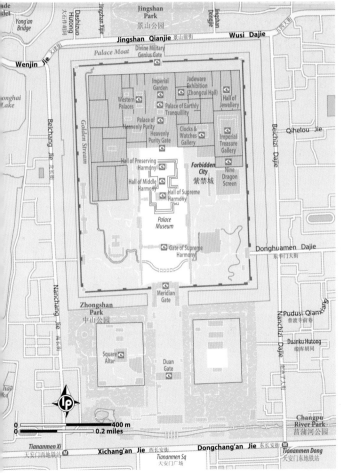

Jingshan Park
景山公园

Jingshan Qianjie 景山前街   Wusi Dajie

Palace Moat   Divine Military
Genius Gate

Wenjin Jie 文津街

Imperial
Garden

Jadeware
Exhibition
(Zhongcui Hall)

Hall of
Jewellery

Western
Palaces

Palace of Earthly
Tranquillity

Qihelou Jie

Palace of
Heavenly Purity

Golden Stream

Heavenly
Purity Gate

Clocks &
Watches
Gallery

Imperial
Treasure
Gallery

Beichizi Dajie

Hall of Preserving
Harmony

Forbidden
City
紫禁城

Nine
Dragon
Screen

Hall of Middle
Harmony

Hall of Supreme
Harmony

Palace
Museum

Donghuamen Dajie
东华门大街

Gate of Supreme
Harmony

Pudusi Qianxiang
普渡寺前巷

Duanku Hutong
缎库胡同

Meridian
Gate

Zhongshan
Park
中山公园

Nanchizi Dajie

Square
Altar

Duan
Gate

Changpu
River Park
菖蒲河公园

0   400 m
0   0.2 miles

Tiananmen Xi Ⓜ
天安门西地铁站

Xichang'an Jie 西长安街

Dongchang'an Jie 东长安街

Tiananmen Dong Ⓜ
天安门东地铁站

Tiananmen Sq
天安门广场

SCAM ALERT!

Most Beijing trips are trouble-free but there are some scams of which visitors should be aware.
Tea Scams Rampant in Beijing, this involves young women or teenagers befriending travellers
(usually couples or single men) and inviting them to a teahouse to chat or practise English.
When the bill comes, the traveller is left with a Y2000 tab (over 100 times the regular price).
The money is later split between the teahouse and the woman who brought the travellers in.
Rickshaw Drivers This one concerns independent rickshaw drivers targeting solo travellers
(women in particular) in touristy areas. After agreeing on a price and taking the Chinese
name-card with the visitor's destination, the driver then throws the card away (leaving
non-Chinese speakers dependent), drives to an isolated location and demands more money.
Several travellers have reported being intimidated by the drivers and at least one woman
was followed back to her hostel and physically threatened when she refused to pay extra.
Art Students Mainly in the Tiananmen Square and Wangfujing Dajie areas, this involves
fake 'art' students inviting travellers to see 'their' exhibition. In reality, the 'art' is often
low-quality, mass-produced knock-offs being sold for outrageous prices.

where Chinese emperors came to
worship their ancestors and the
temple complex inside is one of
Beijing's best-kept secrets.

ZHONGSHAN PARK 中山堂
☎ 6605 4594; Xichang'an Jie, 西长安
街; admission Y2; ⏰ 6am-10pm, last
entry 9pm; ◉ Tiananmen Xi
Now a colourful oasis of greenery
and flowers, emperors once came
here to offer sacrifices to the gods
of land and grain. The square altar
is symmetrical with the Altar of
Ancestors in the Workers' Cultural
Palace (p43) to the east.

SHOP
The pedestrianised Wangfujing
Dajie is a shopping mecca lined
with department stores and mega-

malls. For Tibetan prayer beads and
Buddha effigies, Yonghegong Dajie
outside Lama Temple is excellent.

DRAGON CREATURE
COMICS 龙裔元创动漫店
Collectables
☎ 8402 7166; www.longyicomics
.com; 67 Guozijian Jie, 国子监街67号;
⏰ 9.20am-7pm; ◉ Andingmen
Collectables include T-shirts, mugs,
action figures and stuffed animals,
all boasting the images of Asian
animation icons. Japanese, Chinese
and Korean comics line the shelves.

FOREIGN LANGUAGES
BOOKSTORE 外文书店 *Books*
☎ 6512 6911; 235 Wangfujing Dajie,
王府井大街235号; ⏰ 9am-10pm;
◉ Wangfujing

Shelves here groan with English fiction, Chinese literature in translation, Lonely Planets, and the best range of 'Learn Chinese' materials in the city.

PLASTERED T-SHIRTS
创可贴T-恤 *Clothing*

☎ 139 102 05721; www.plastered.com.cn; 61 Nanluogu Xiang, 南锣鼓巷61号; ⏱ 10am-10pm; Ⓜ Andingmen
Wonder where everybody's got their 'Beijing Subway' T-shirt from? This is the place. Local icons are slapped on T-shirts (Y80 to Y100) in a tongue-in-cheek way that gets expats and locals laughing out loud at the in-jokes.

SANSHIZHAI KITES
三石斋风筝 *Toys*

☎ 8404 4505; www.cnkites.com; 25 Dianmen Xidajie, 地安门西大街25号; ⏱ 10am-9pm; Ⓜ Andingmen, then taxi
This family-owned business sells a gorgeous array of homemade silk and bamboo kites. Choose from sectioned dragon kites and massive butterfly contraptions, which they say soar over 1000m.

SHENGTANGXUAN
盛唐轩 *Toys*

☎ 8404 7179; www.rbtys.com in Chinese; 38 Guozijian Jie, 国子监街38号; ⏱ 9am-7pm; Ⓜ Andingmen
This little shop (keep an eye out for the giant toy statue outside)

has a fascinating display of traditional Chinese toys. Just take the staff's claims that items are all 'traditional old Beijing toys' with a grain of salt; some are native to, and made in, other regions of China.

TEN FU'S TEA 天福茗茶
Souvenirs

☎ 6524 0958; www.tenfu.com in Chinese; Wangfujing Dajie, 王府井大街; ⏱ 9am-11pm; Ⓜ Wangfujing
This Taiwanese chain sells countless sorts of loose tea and all manner of tea accessories. Wangfujing is its biggest Beijing branch so there's always plenty of free tastings and samples.

Handle with care

DISTRICTS

DONGCHENG

🍴 EAT

🍴 BAGUO BUYI 巴国布衣
Sichuan YY

☎ 6400 8888; 89-3 Dianmen Dongdajie, 地安门东大街89-3号; ⏰ 11am-2pm & 5-9.30pm; ⊛ Andingmen, then taxi
Colourful and theatrical, this place is done up like a Chinese inn. The food is excellent with staples like tofu and chilli and crispy mandarin fish. Night entertainment often includes *bian lian* (a dazzling Sichuan face-change performance). English menu available.

🍴 CAFÉ SAMBAL
Southeast Asian YY

☎ 6400 4875; 43 Doufuchi Hutong (off Jiugulou Dajie), 旧鼓楼大街豆腐池胡同43号; ⏰ 11am-midnight; ⊛ Gulou Dajie; ⓥ
Sparse, eccentric decoration means you could be sitting on anything from a bright-orange couch to a high table or a squat stool. Malaysian curries are the standouts here, especially the chicken varieties. English menu available.

🍴 COURTYARD 四合院
Fusion YYY

☎ 6526 8883; 95 Donghuamen Dajie, 东华门大街95号; ⏰ 6-10pm; ⊛ Tiananmen Dong, then taxi
As if the dining room overlooking the Forbidden City's moat wasn't enough, this restaurant boasts one of the best wine lists in Beijing and an ever-changing fusion menu that combines Asian and European flavours. English menu available.

🍴 DONGHUAMEN NIGHT MARKET 东华门夜市 *Snacks* Y

Donganmen Dajie, 东安门大街; ⏰ 5.30-10.30pm; ⊛ Wangfujing
Dozens of stalls are thrown up here each evening selling a kaleidoscopic choice of skewered grasshoppers and scorpions alongside more familiar fare like noodles and fruit kebabs. It's a sight in and of itself.

🍴 MADE IN CHINA 长安一号
Beijing/Peking Duck YYY

☎ 8518 1234, ext 3608; Grand Hyatt, Dongchang'an Jie, 东长安街北京东方君悦大酒店; ⏰ 11.30am-2.30pm & 5.30-10pm; ⊛ Wangfujing
One of the Grand Hyatt's standout restaurants, this is an excellent choice for those that want traditional Beijing dishes in an upscale atmosphere. Try the Peking Duck, its hallmark dish.

🍴 QUANJUDE ROAST DUCK RESTAURANT 全聚德烤鸭店
Peking Duck YY

☎ 6525 3310; 9 Shuaifuyuan Hutong, 帅府园胡同9号; ⏰ 11am-2pm & 4.30-9pm; ⊛ Wangfujing
This is the best branch of this historic (and now slightly kitschy)

roast-duck chain. Long lines are par for the course but ultra-efficient staff keep things moving. Classic roast duck shares the menu with appetisers such as duck wings with red yeast and spicy duck tongue. English menu available.

🍴 RED CAPITAL CLUB 新红资俱乐部 *Imperial/Beijing* YYY
☎ 6402 7150, 8401 8866; 66 Dongsi Jiutiao, 东四九条66号; ⏱ 6-11pm; ❻ Dongsishitiao

With its 1950s Politburo-meeting props, this restored Qing-styled courtyard is high camp at its best. Dishes aren't so much listed on the menu as leisurely revealed in pages of coy, poem-sized prose. Reservations are required.

🍴 SOURCE 都江源 *Sichuan* YYY
☎ 6400 3736; 14 Banchang Hutong, 板厂胡同14号; ⏱ 11am-2pm & 5.30-10.30pm; ❻ Andingmen, then taxi

A true gastronomic treat, this courtyard restaurant serves two daily set menus (Y158 for one built around meat and chicken; Y238 for one built around fish and shrimp). These multicourse meals are served in small, elegant portions punched up with Sichuan flavours and spices. Service is outstanding whether you're a solo diner or with a group. Food allergies and preferences are cheerfully accommodated.

🍴 WANGFUJING SNACK STREET 王府井小吃街 *Snacks* Y
Wangfujing Dajie, 王府井大街; ⏱ 11am-8pm; ❻ Wangfujing

This pedestrianised street just off Wangfujing Dajie is a jumble of atmosphere and flavour. Stalls are bursting with food from all over China, including flat bread, oodles of noodles and pancakes.

🍴 XIAN BAI WEI 鲜百味 *Regional Chinese* Y
☎ 6402 7070; 76 Yonghegong Dajie, 雍和宫大街76号; ⏱ 11am-10pm; ❻ Beixinqiao

This family-run Shaanxi joint has a picture-menu you can choose your snacks from. Try the *rojiamo*

THE GHOST STREET STROLL

Affectionately called 'Ghost Street', one section of Dongzhimennei Dajie (Map pp40–1, D3) is decorated with hundreds of red lanterns and is completely lined on both sides by restaurants ranging from cheap Chongqing-style hotpot places to bustling sit-down dining rooms. It's a favourite local hangout on Friday and Saturday nights with crazy crowds and a fantastic atmosphere. Nobody knows exactly where this drag got its peculiar name; some say it's because all the lanterns remind people of a ghost festival, others say it's a tip of the hat to the restaurants' all-night opening hours.

(a kind of Shaanxi sandwich, Y3.50) with shredded pork between a ricepaper-like bun. It has no English sign or building number outside. The entrance is next to the clothing store at 74 Yonghegong Dajie.

🍴 XU XIANG ZHAI VEGETARIAN RESTAURANT

叙香斋 *Vegetarian* Y

☎ 6404 6568; 26 Guozijian Jie, 国子监街26号; ⏰ 11.30am-2pm & 5.30-9pm; ⊕ Yonghegong-Lama Temple;

A favourite with Buddhist monks, the fishless sushi and meatless Chinese dishes are so authentic, you can't tell they're vegetarian. Go for the buffet (Y58) and sample veggie versions of over three-dozen classic Chinese dishes. Staff are equally welcoming whether you're dining solo or in a group.

🍸 DRINK

🍸 BED BAR 床吧 *Bar*

☎ 8400 1554; 17 Zhangwang Hutong, Jiugulou Dajie, 旧鼓楼大街张旺胡同17号; ⏰ 4pm-2am Mon & Tue, noon-late Wed-Sun; ⊕ Gulou Dajie

A wicked layout of interconnected rooms and kang-style floor seating has made this bar the big new favourite. The entrance isn't always marked. To find the right door, walk 40m down the *hutong* from Jiugulou Dajie and listen for the music.

🍸 DRUM & BELL

钟鼓咖啡馆 *Bar*

☎ 8403 3600; 41 Zhonglouwan Hutong, 钟楼湾胡同41号; ⏰ noon-2am; ⊕ Gulou Dajie

In the alley between the Drum and Bell Towers (p39), this bar's staff is among the friendliest in town. The comfy rooftop terrace is loaded with couches and armchairs, and in summer regulars camp out here till closing. Wi-fi hotspot.

🍸 PASSBY BAR 过客酒吧 *Bar*

☎ 8403 8004; www.passbybar.com; 108 Nanluogu Xiang, 南锣鼓巷108号; ⏰ 9am-2pm; ⊕ Andingmen, then taxi

This travel-oriented bar with its 'hang-out-in-the-living-room-and-chat-with-your-buddies'

Work on your neon tan around Houhai Lake (p120)

vibe attracts locals, expats and those just passing through. Don't confuse this with the new, slightly more upscale **Passby Restaurant** (☎ 6400 6868; 114 Nanluogu Xiang, 南锣鼓巷114号; ⏰ 11am-midnight) down the street.

 # PLAY

⭐ **MAO LIVEHOUSE** 光芒
Live Music
☎ 6402 5080; www.maolive.com; 111 **Gulou Dongdaji,** 鼓楼东大街111号; ⏰ **8pm-late;** Ⓜ **Andingmen**
Considered the best live venue in Beijing, local jazz, death-metal and even Britpop-style bands regularly take to Mao's stage. No matter who's playing, Mao is almost exclusively packed with the same music-mad Beijingers, and rubbing elbows with them is often just as interesting as watching what's on stage.

⭐ **HEPING FOOT MASSAGE 81** 和平健身81 *Massage*
☎ 6522 8355; 3 Jinyu Hutong, beside **Taiwan Hotel,** 金鱼胡同3号台湾饭店旁; **massages from Y110;** ⏰ **8am-2am;** Ⓜ **Wangfujing**
Heping's reputation was made on its luxury foot massages. Complimentary watermelon, a plasma TV broadcasting English-language satellite programming and a cocktail menu are among the perks.

>NORTH CHAOYANG 朝阳北

Chaoyang is Beijing's biggest district, and its northern section is the dedicated stomping ground of local foodies, clubbers and shopaholics. North Chaoyang's embassy district is a lovely area with clean wide boulevards, trees and greenery. The foreign embassy staff powers North Chaoyang's excellent choice of international restaurants and speciality shops.

Sanlitun Lu, once the city's main bar street, is also here. Now crowded with generic bars, it's the clubs and pubs hidden in the surrounding lanes and nearby streets that draw people from all over Beijing. Terrific nightlife and massive dance clubs crowd around the Workers' Stadium southeast of here.

Though there's not a lot in the way of formal sights, the Taoist Dongyue Temple, with its cast of demons, is definitely among the most memorable. Olympic Park is in the far north of the district and is where you'll find the headline-making Bird's Nest stadium (p17).

NORTH CHAOYANG

Please see over for map

SEE

C5ART 西五画廊

☎ 6460 3950; www.C5Art.com; 5 Sanlitun Xiwujie, 三里屯西五 街5号; ⏰ 10am-7pm Tue-Sun; Ⓜ Dongzhimen, then taxi

This gallery was established to showcase up-and-coming artists, including those working in less common areas like new media. To get here, follow the sign from Sanlitun Xiwujie down the alley to the SOS Health Clinic. There'll be a C5Art sign here pointing you the rest of the way.

DONGYUE TEMPLE 东岳庙

☎ 6551 0151;141 Chaoyangmenwai Dajie, 朝阳门外大街141号; adult/child Y10/5; ⏰ 8.30am-5pm 1 May-31 Sep, last entry 4.30pm; Ⓜ Chaoyangmen exit A, then taxi

Hundreds of life-sized ghoul and ghost statues populate the Dongyue Temple, a Taoist temple that honours the God of Taishan (one of China's holy mountains). These figures await you (and your offerings), ready to help with everything from financial gain to protection from harassment in the netherworld.

POLY ART MUSEUM 保利艺术博物馆

New Poly Plaza, Chaoyangmen Beidajie, 新保利大厦, 朝阳门北大街; admission Y50; ⏰ 9.30am-4.30pm Tue, Thu & Sat, group reservations Mon, Wed & Fri; Ⓜ Dongsishitiao

This museum has the most beautifully presented collections of bronzes and Buddha effigies in Beijing. The Poly Group bought the exhibits at international auctions in order to 'return them to the motherland'. The museum will be at the address given here by the time you're in town.

OLYMPIC PARK 奥林匹克公园

Beisanhuan Zhonglu, 北三环中路; Ⓜ Gulou Dajie, then taxi

Way up in the north of the district, the Olympic Green is one of Beijing's biggest green spaces, developed for the 2008 Olympics. Nearly a dozen venues are being set up here especially for the

NORTH CHAOYANG

China Culture Club ■

1 km
0.5 miles
0

To
Kolegas
(200m)

Chaoyang
Park
朝阳公园

To Olympic
Park (0.5km)

Xibahe Nanlu

Tai Shu Xi
Restaurant
(4km)

Xiba River 西坝河

Liufang Jie

Zuojiazhuang Beixiejie

Zuojiazhuang Xijie

Zuojiazhuang Xijie

Baisanhuan Donglu 北三环东路

Dongsanhuan Beilu

Sanyuan Qiao
(under construction)
三元桥站

Xiaoyun Lu

Liangmaqiao Lu

Kempinski Hotel;
Jinghua Wushu
Association

Liangmahe
(under construction)
亮马桥站

Liangma River 亮马河

Xinyuan Nanlu

Shuyuan Nanlu

Baijiazhuang Donglie
白家庄东街

Baijiazhuang Dongjie

Xinyuan Jie

Xinyuan Jie

Xin Donglu

Dangzhimenwai Xiejie

Xiangheyuan Lu

Dongzhimenwai Zhongjie
东直门外中街

Dongzhimenwai Xiejie 东直门外斜街

Dongzhimenwai Xinyuanxiti Zhongjie

Dongzhimenwai Dajie 东直门外大街

Dongzhimen Beidajie
东直门北大街

Dongsanhuan Beilu 东三环北路

Nongzhanguan
农业展览馆站

Agricultural
Exhibition
Center

Sanlitun Nanlu

Sanlitun Dongsijie

Sanlitun Dongwujie

Sanlitun Xiliujie

Sanlitun Xinwujie

Sanlitun Beixiaojie

SANLITUN
EMBASSY
AREA

Sanlitun Lu 三里屯路

Canadian
Embassy ●

Australian
Embassy ●

CHAOYANG

Chuxin Lu

Xingfucun Lu

Sanlitun Dongsijie

Sanlitun Dongsanjie

Sanlitun Dong'erjie

French Embassy ●

Dongzhong Jie

4

1

2

3

4

10

13

15

16

18

19

20

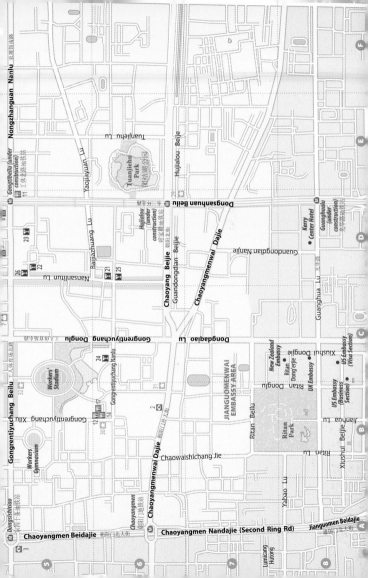

WORTH THE TRIP: FACTORY 798/DASHANZI ART DISTRICT 大山子艺术区

Factory 798, also called the Dashanzi Art District, sits in northeastern Chaoyang; see p16. Some of the most important galleries here include **White Space Gallery** (☎ 8456 2054; www .alexanderochs-galleries.de; Factory 798, 2 Jiuxianqiao Lu, 酒仙桥路2号大山子艺术区; ☉ noon-6pm), specialising in Chinese and contemporary art from abroad, and **Beijing Commune** (☎ 8654 9428; www.beijingcommune.com; Seven Star Rd, 七星路; ☉ 11am-7pm Tue-Sun), devoted to experimental art and run by art-scene bad boy Leng Lin. **798 Photo Gallery** (☎ 6438 1784; www.798photogallery.cn; Ceramics Third Street, 陶瓷三街; ☉ 10am-6pm) is a dynamic place to check out contemporary photography from China.

Factory 798 also houses **Timezone 8 Art Books** (☎ 8456 0336; www.timezone8.com; 798 Rd, 798路; ☉ 10am-9pm), which has Beijing's best selection of books (in all languages) on Chinese contemporary art and artists, as well as titles on world art, architecture and design.

Several cafés, bars and restaurants hide among the galleries. Many of these eateries have stunning interior design. **Café Pause** (☎ 6431 6214; 797 Rd, 797 路; ☉ 10am-9pm) is dark and moody with a menu heavy on Eastern European fare. Elsewhere, **Jiang Hu Club** (☎ 6431 5190; 798 Rd, 798 路; ☉ 11am-11pm) serves mainly Italian and French dishes and is the most upscale restaurant in the area.

Games, including two of Beijing's most iconic new buildings, the Bird's Nest and the Water Cube (see p103 and p17), both of which are worth the trip just to see from the outside.

SHOP

JAYI CLOTHING MARKET 佳亿时尚广场
Clothing/Market

Xinyuan Nanlu, 新源南路昆仑饭店对面**;** ⏲ **9.30am-9pm;** ⊕ **Dongzhimen, then taxi**
Come to this market for great prices, friendly bargaining and a taste of what it was like at Yaxiu Clothing Market (right) and the Silk Market (p76) before they got popular. It's across from the Kunlun Hotel.

ROUGE BAISER
Clothing/Homewares

☎ **6464 3530; www.rougebaiser-elise .com; 5 Sanlitun Xiwujie,** 三里屯西五街5号**;** ⏲ **10am-7pm Mon-Sat, 11am-5pm Sun;** ⊕ **Dongzhimen, then taxi**
Gorgeous sheets, kids' clothes and homewares are sold here, all created by a Shanghai-based French designer. Many items, including the cotton-linen bedspread sets, are embroidered with Chinese-influenced designs like kites.

WUZHOU FRIENDSHIP SILK TRADE COMPANY 五洲友谊丝绸贸易公司 *Clothing*

☎ **6532 7913; 2nd fl Friendship Supermarket, 7 Sanlitun Lu,** 三里屯路7号,友谊超市2层**;** ⏲ **10.30am-8.30pm;** ⊕ **Dongzhimen, then taxi**
Located in the embassy district, this tailor/material store is familiar with foreigners and 'foreigner' sizes and styles. *Qipao* (figure-hugging Chinese-style dresses) and men's shirts take two to three days.

YAXIU CLOTHING MARKET 三里屯雅秀市场
Clothing/Market

☎ **6416 8945; Gongrentiyuchang Beilu,** 工人体育场北路**;** ⏲ **9.30am-9pm;** ⊕ **Dongsishitiao, then taxi**
Along with South Chaoyang's Silk Market (p76), this is a travellers' favourite for clothes, outdoor gear, shoes and bags. Bargains aren't as common here as they once were so haggle hard!

EAT

1001 NIGHTS 1001夜
Middle Eastern

☎ **6532 4050; www.1001nights.com.cn; Gongrentiyuchang Beilu,** 工人体育场北路**;** ⏲ **11am-2pm;** ⊕ **Dongsishitiao, then taxi;** V
This place has a cavernous dining area, friendly waitstaff and nightly belly dancing to go along with its

Tian Yuan
Director, White Space Gallery (p56)

How do you pick artists for the gallery? It's never the same thing. The work just has to move me somehow, then I think 'OK, let's take a closer look at this'. **What's going on in Chinese contemporary art these days?** Artists born in the '70s and '80s saw so much societal change, a lot of that is expressed in their work. Those born in the late '80s and early '90s are fuelled more by the personal. You don't necessarily see as many political themes in their work. **What's special about Beijing's art scene?** It's a real community. Artists in Beijing always stick close to each other, they work together, live together, hang out together. You don't see the same kind of thing in places like Shanghai. **What is it about Beijing that unleashes so much creativity?** It's big, lively, multi-faceted. It's only natural that it fuels artists' lives and artists' work.

extensive menu of Middle Eastern specialities like *merguez* (spicy sausage) platters. English menu available.

🍴 ALAMEDA *Fusion* YY
☎ 6417 8084; alameda_beijing@yahoo.com; Sanlitun Beijie, 三里屯北街; ⏱ noon-3pm & 5-10.30pm; Ⓜ Dongsishitiao, then taxi
Alameda's Brazilian chef incorporates ingredients from South America, Asia and Europe in her ever-changing set menus. The conservatory-style dining room is flooded with natural light. English menu available.

🍴 APRIL GOURMET
绿叶子食品店 *Deli* Y
☎ 8455 1245; 1 Sanlitun Beixiaojie, 三里屯北小街; ⏱ 8am-9pm; Ⓜ Dongzhimen, then taxi
This is an excellent place for cold cuts, cheeses and wines in the heart of the embassy district.

🍴 BEIJING DADONG ROAST DUCK RESTAURANT 北京大董烤鸭店 *Peking Duck* YY
☎ 6582 2892; Dongsanhuan Beilu, 东三环北路; ⏱ 11am-10pm; Ⓜ Dongsishitiao, then taxi
Many consider this to be the best duck restaurant in Beijing. It has a staggering array of fowl to choose from, including the foreigner-friendly 'super-lean'.

Dining rooms range from standard Chinese pomp to elaborate champagne-coloured tablecloths and settings. Staff can be brisk, but with lines snaking out the door, who can blame them? English menu available.

🍴 BELLAGIO 鹿港小镇
North Asian Y
☎ 6551 3533; 6 Gongrentiyuchang Xilu, 工人体育场西路6号; ⏱ 11am-5am; Ⓜ Dongsishitiao, then taxi
The nightclub vibe and spiky-haired waitstaff (yep, the hairstyle is part of the job) set this hip eatery apart from its competitors. Come between midnight and dawn and it will be packed with clubbers tucking into Bellagio's famous *baobing* desserts made from shaved ice, fruit, nuts and condensed milk.

🍴 DIN TAI FUNG 鼎泰丰
Regional Chinese Y
☎ 6462 4502; www.dintaifung.com.cn; 24 Xinyuanxili Zhongjie, 源源西里中街24号; ⏱ 11.30am-2.30pm & 5-10pm Mon-Fri, 11am-10pm Sat & Sun; Ⓜ Dongzhimen, then taxi
Bright and minimalist with (almost) floor-to-ceiling windows, Din Tai Fung is a friendly restaurant that specialises in noodles and its star dish: seafood dumplings. Reservations are advised for Friday and Saturday

nights. The 2nd floor is nonsmoking. English menu available.

⅄⅃ GREEN T HOUSE 紫云轩
Fusion YYY

☎ 6552 8310; 6 Gongrentiyuchang Xilu, 工人体育场西路6号; ⏱ 10.30am-2.30pm & 6pm-midnight; Ⓜ Dongsishitiao, then taxi

We could describe the soaring white walls, high-backed chairs and eye-popping décor for hours, but you would still need to come see it for yourself. The cuisine is best described as Asian fusion with tea somehow worked into almost every dish. Reservations are advisable. English menu available.

⅄⅃ HAITANGHUA PYONGYANG COLD NOODLE RESTAURANT 平壤海棠花冷面馆
North Asian YY

☎ 6461 6295/6298; 8 Xinyuanxili Zhongjie, 新源西里中街8号; ⏱ 11.30am-2.30pm & 5-10.30pm; Ⓜ Dongzhimen, then taxi

As if opening a 'North Korean' restaurant wasn't enough of a lure, this eatery gets its severe, black-clad waitresses to break out into Korean folk-songs between servings. The picture menu is heavy on Korean hotpot and, of course, noodles. The restaurant is on the corner of Xin Donglu.

⅄⅃ LE BISTROT PARISIEN 巴黎乐事多餐厅
European YY

☎ 6417 8188; bistrotparisien@sina.com; 1f Tongli Bldg, Sanlitun Jie, 三里屯街同里1层; ⏱ 11am-11pm; Ⓜ Dongsishitiao, then taxi

This restaurant has traditional French *bistrot* décor and an able French chef who flawlessly weaves local flavours into classic French dishes from the entrees down to desserts like pineapple crème brûlée. English menu available.

⅄⅃ TAI SHU XI 太熟悉
Chinese Homestyle Y

☎ 6491 0368; Huixin Dongjie, 惠新东街; ⏱ 11am-2pm & 5-10.30pm; Ⓜ Yonghegong-Lama Temple, then taxi

Dishes are beautifully presented at this fantastic (and *very* boisterous) neighbourhood eatery. It also does a terrific Peking duck with unusual condiments like melon and pumpkin-flavoured pancakes. English menu available.

⅄⅃ THREE GUIZHOU MEN 三个贵州人
Regional Chinese Y

☎ 6551 8517; Gongrentiyuchang Xilu, 工人体育场西路; ⏱ 24hr; Ⓜ Dongsishitiao, then taxi

Spicy ribs and sour-fish hotpot are two of this restaurant's star dishes from Guizhou province. The restaurant's trendy decoration features local artwork and the service is excellent. To get here, walk down the lane behind Bellagio (p59) until you see the hostess with the silver headdress. She'll stick you in an elevator and zip you up to the restaurant on the 2nd floor. See also the boxed text, p91.

XIANGMANLOU 香满楼
Peking Duck Y

☎ 6467 4391; Xinyuanxili Zhongjie, 新源西里中街; ⏰ 11am-10pm; ⓜ Dongzhimen, then taxi

If you want your Peking duck experience to come without tourist trappings, navigate your way to this popular neighbourhood hangout for a quality duck.

XINJIANG RED ROSE RESTAURANT 新疆红玫瑰餐厅
Muslim Y

☎ 6415 5741; 5 Xingfuyicun, 工人体育场北门对面,幸福一村5号; ⏰ 11am-11pm; ⓜ Dongsishitiao, then taxi

Eating here is like hanging out at a raucous party. Communal seating is at long canteen-style tables, and when the Uighur music and dancers take to the floor between 7pm and 8pm nightly – look out! Choose from any of the menu's excellent mutton dishes. It's opposite the north gate of the Workers' Stadium.

DRINK

BAR BLU 蓝吧 *Bar*

☎ 6417 4142; www.barblu.com.cn; 4th fl, Tongli Studios, Sanlitun Beijie, 三里屯北街同里4层; ⏰ 4pm-late; ⓜ Dongsishitiao, then taxi

Wednesday Quiz Night is this bar's signature event. Otherwise you can choose from its dance floor, lounge or gorgeous rooftop terrace. Don't miss its Flaming Lamborghini cocktail – five 'secret' liqueurs stacked in three separate glasses and set alight for Y70.

BEER MANIA 麦霓啤酒吧 *Bar*

☎ 6585 0786; 1st fl, Taiyue Hotel, Nansanlitun Lu, 南三里屯路泰悦豪庭1层; ⏰ 2pm-late; ⓜ Dongsishitiao, then taxi

Over 70 kinds of Belgian beers are on offer in this cosy pub, including Hoegaarden on draught (Y45). Happy hour is 5pm to 7pm.

▼ BOOKWORM 书虫 *Café*
☎ 6586 9507; www.beijingbookworm .com; Nansanlitun Lu, 南三里屯路; ☽ 9am-1am; ◎ Dongsishitiao, then taxi

This English-language lending library is a hub of expat life in Beijing. Author talks, current affairs lectures and other China-related events are regularly scheduled. Food, coffee and cocktails are served all day. This is a wi-fi hotspot.

▼ BROWNS *Bar*
☎ 6591 2717; Nansanlitun Lu, 南三 里屯路; ☽ 11am-2am Mon, Tue, Thu & Sun, 11am-4am Wed, Fri & Sat; ◎ Dongsishitiao, then taxi

The dull name doesn't do this bar justice. It's a remarkable place where business people hang out alongside club kids. DJs play house and rock music most nights while Tuesday is 'Texas American Singer' night.

Fund your Beijing visit shooting pool at the Rickshaw

▼ PIPE'S CAFÉ 啤酒层 *Bar*

☎ 6593 7756; Workers' Stadium south gate, 工人体育场南门; ⏰ 6pm-2am; ◉ Chaoyangmen, then taxi

Nothing special during the week, but everything changes on Saturday when it's lesbian night. The dance floor is tiny but the turnout is usually good with everyone moving on to Destination (p65) after midnight. The Saturday cover charge is Y30.

▼ Q BAR Q吧 *Bar*

☎ 6595 9239; www.qbarbeijing.com; Nansanlitun Lu, 南三里屯路; ⏰ 6pm-2am; ◉ Dongsishitiao, then taxi

Unselfconsciously cool, Q has terrific bartenders and the best rooftop terrace in town and is packed with interesting people on weekends. To get here, go to the Eastern Inn Hotel, take the elevator to the 5th floor, turn right and walk up the 6th-floor staircase.

▼ RICKSHAW 人力车酒吧 *Bar*

☎ 6500 4330; Sanlitun Nanlu, 三里屯南路; ⏰ 24hr; ◉ Donsishitiao, then taxi

This small bar has an upper floor with loud music and a pool table, a quieter downstairs with bright-orange couches, and a small outside sitting area. Besides round-the-clock drinks, the bar food here is terrific, especially the Tex-Mex stuff like burritos and quesadillas.

KARAOKE

Karaoke bars (signed 'KTV') are everywhere. Renting a room with your friends and wailing out the hits is the way most Beijingers like to spend their weekends. Because it goes on in private rooms, it can be a hard scene for visitors to crack – who wants to rent a room and sing to themselves? But if you want to check some out for yourself, **Melody** (☎ 6551 0808; A-77 Chaoyangmenwai Dajie; rooms per hr from Y109; ⏰ 8am-2am) is a popular place and you might be able to split a room with some locals and get them to show you what all the fuss is about.

⭐ PLAY

⭐ 2 KOLEGAS 两个好朋友

Live Music

☎ 8196 4820; www.2kolegas.com; 21 Liangmaqiao Lu, 亮马桥路21号 (汽车电影院内); ⏰ 7.30pm-late; ◉ Dongzhimen, then taxi

Underground rock and punk acts rule at this ramshackle but super-friendly club, which offers enticing Y20-pitchers of beer. It's inside a drive-in movie theatre – to get here head about 1500m down the driveway from Liangmaqiao Lu. The bar is hidden behind the big colourful restaurant to the left of the drive-in.

Rooftop relaxation at World of Suzie Wong

⭐ BEIJING CD JAZZ CAFÉ 北京 CD 士俱乐 部 *Live Music*
☎ 6506 8288; 16 Dongsanhuan Beilu, 东三环北16路; 🕐 4pm-late; 🚇 Dongzhimen, then taxi

This is a great no-frills club with jazz-funk on Saturday, a swing night on Monday and classic jazz or big-band groups the rest of the week. The bar's just behind the overpass south of the Agricultural Exhibition Center.

⭐ BODHI 菩提会所 *Massage*
☎ 6417 9595; www.bodhi.com.cn; 17 Gongrentiyuchang Beilu, 工人体育场北路17号(体育场北门对面); 🕐 11am-12.30am; 🚇 Donsishitiao, then taxi

A favourite with locals from nearby embassies, this upscale spa centre has Asian-influenced decoration and an extensive menu of massage styles, wraps and facials. Two-hour spa packages range from Y500 to Y600. It's opposite the north gate of the Workers' Stadium.

⭐ CHAOYANG THEATRE 朝阳 剧场 *Acrobatics/Peking Opera*
☎ 6507 2421; 36 Dongsanhuan Beilu, 东三环北路36号; tickets Y180-580; 🚇 Chaoyangmen

Thrilling acrobatic performances are staged in the grand hall while a small faux 'teahouse' is set upstairs for boisterous Peking operas. There are 75-minute acrobatic performances at 5.15pm and 7.15pm and one-hour Peking opera performances at 7.20pm.

⭐ DESTINATION 目的地 *Club*
☎ 6551 5138; www.bjdestination.com; 7 Gongrentiyuchang Xilu, 工人体育场西路7号; cover charge Y30; ☽ 6pm-late; Ⓜ Dongsishitiao, then taxi
This grey, concrete block is *the* gay club in Beijing. As any local will tell you, Destination is beloved for the clientele it draws, not the dismal interior design. There's a Y30 to Y40 cover charge on Friday and Saturday nights.

⭐ MIX 密克斯 *Club*
☎ 6530 2889; inside Workers' Stadium north gate, 工人体育场北门内; ☽ 8pm-late; Ⓜ Dongsishitiao, then taxi
Fashionable Beijingers line up for hours to get into this hip-hop and R&B dance club on weekends. Star DJs from Asia and abroad pack the club for the rest of the week.

⭐ WORLD OF SUZIE WONG 苏西黄 *Club*
☎ 6593 7889; www.suziewong.com.cn; 1A Nongzhanguan Nanlu, 农展馆路甲1号; ☽ 7pm-late; Ⓜ Dongsishitiao, then taxi
Recently reopened after renovations, Suzie Wong's décor still screams Shanghai opium-den and attracts Beijing's most beautiful people with house, techno, pop and rock. Get here early if you want one of the kang-style, low-level beds stacked with pillows. The club entrance is south of Chaoyang Park. Suzie is on the 2nd floor.

>CHONGWEN 崇文

Chongwen may not have as many attention-grabbing attractions as some of Beijing's other districts, but what it does have packs an unforgettable punch. The Temple of Heaven Park, a darling of postcard photographers and a visitor favourite, occupies a huge chunk of the district's west side. Nearby, the Pearl Market draws hordes of shoppers looking for deals on rings, necklaces and semiprecious stones. Despite losing many of its courtyard neighbourhoods, pockets of traditional life still remain in Chongwen. Check out the district's northwest section where there's a vibrant *hutong* (alleyway) area bordered by Qianmen Dajie, Qinian Dajie, Zhushikou Dajie and Qianmen Dongdajie. Elsewhere, Chongwen is generally (by Beijing terms anyway) low key. While the rest of the city erupts in skyscrapers, glitzy shops and daring design, Chongwen, located southeast of Tiananmen Square, remains much the same as it always has been, with wide dusty roads and faded buildings in various states of disrepair.

CHONGWEN

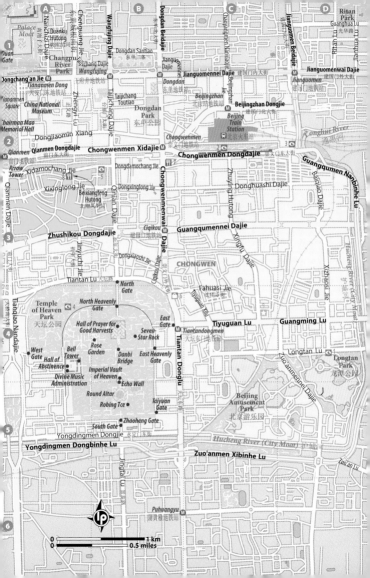

SEE

◎ LONGTAN PARK 龙潭公园

☎ 6716 7319; Longtan Lu, 龙潭路; admission Y2; ⏰ 6am-10pm, last entry 9pm; ◉ Tiantandongmen, then taxi

Activities are tucked in every corner of this park, including outdoor gyms (with English instructions for the equipment), ping-pong tables and a beautiful jogging track that weaves through the greenery.

◎ MING CITY WALL RUINS PARK 明城墙遗址公园

Chongwenmen Dongdajie, 崇文门东大街; admission free; ⏰ 24hr; ◉ Chongwenmen or Jianguomen

The Ming city wall once protected Beijing from the outside world. Most of the fortification is long gone, except for here, where a charming park has been built along a restored section of the structure. Excellent English captions along the footpath explain the wall's history.

◎ RED GATE GALLERY 红门画廊

☎ 6525 1005; www.redgategallery .com; Dongbianmen, 东便门; ⏰ 10am-5pm; ◉ Jianguomen or Chongwenmen

Opened in 1991 in a stunning watchtower setting (see Southeast Watchtower, right), Red Gate has been one of the most influential modern and contemporary art galleries ever since. Exhibits are located on the tower's 1st and 4th floors and you usually don't need to pay the tower's admission fee to visit.

◎ SOUTHEAST WATCHTOWER 东南角楼

☎ 8512 1554; Dongbianmen, 东便门; admission Y15; ⏰ 9am-5pm; ◉ Jianguomen or Chongwenmen

This old Ming watchtower has 144 archer windows and reams of 'I was here' graffiti left by international troops during the Boxer Rebellion. On the tower's 2nd and 3rd floors there are historical exhibits about Chongwen district. With the admission ticket, you're allowed to walk the old city wall attached to the tower. If only visiting Red Gate

---

THE GREENING OF QIANMEN DAJIE

While Olympics organisers consider bringing the marathon route along Qianmen Dajie, the street is getting heaps of pre-Games attention. South of Zhushikou Dongdajie, old homes and businesses have been torn down to make way for new 'TV-friendly' plants and grassy spaces. North of Zhushikou Dongdajie, Qianmen Dajie has been sealed off while construction workers supposedly transform it into an 'old-style' pedestrian shopping street. The final results should be unveiled by spring 2008.

Temple of Heaven – if only there were more detail!

Gallery (see opposite), you usually don't need to pay.

TEMPLE OF HEAVEN PARK
天坛公园

☎ 6701 2483; North Gate, Tiantan Donglu, 天坛东路北门; **park & temple complex Y35, park only Y15, Divine Music Administration Y10;** ⏲ **sights 8am-6pm, last entry 5pm, park 6am-9pm, last entry 8pm;** Ⓜ **Tiantandongmen**

From 1420 until the fall of imperial China, this is where successive emperors came with their entourages to pray for good harvests. Nowadays, it's one of those rare places that's equally popular with both travellers and locals. From 6am daily, hundreds of neighbourhood residents swarm here, turning the park grounds into a monster taichi class, while later in the day out-of-town visitors flock here for a chance to ogle the iconic Hall of Prayer for Good Harvests in person. See also p18. Audio guides are Y40.

UNDERGROUND CITY
地下城

☎ 6702 2657; 62 Xidamochang Jie, 西打磨厂街62号; **admission Y20;** ⏲ **8am-6pm;** Ⓜ **Qianmen or Chongwenmen**

In 1969, Mao decided Beijing needed an underground labyrinth where he could send the population (all five million of them) in the event of a nuclear attack by the Soviet Union. Combat-clad guides (most with basic English) now give 20-minute tours through the subterranean trenches.

SHOP

PEARL MARKET 红桥市场
Market

☎ 6713 3354; 16 Hongqiao Lu, 红桥路 16号; ⌚ 8.30am-7pm; Ⓜ Chongwenmen, then taxi

Head straight to the 3rd floor of this multifloored emporium to see the pearls this market is famous for. Every colour and shape you can imagine will be on sale here somewhere. Prices vary wildly de-

pending on quality. Upscale pearl boutiques, patrolled by security guards, are on the 4th floor.

EAT

BIANYIFANG ROAST DUCK RESTAURANT 便宜坊烤鸭店
Peking Duck　　　　　　　　　YY

☎ 6712 0505; 2a Chongwenmenwai Dajie, 崇文门外大街甲2号; ⌚ 11am-10pm; Ⓜ Chongwenmen

Bianyifang's atmosphere is noisy, worn and bustling, but you won't care because this popular Qing-era duck specialist serves a sinfully rich bird with all the trimmings: pancakes, onions, cucumber, sauce, duck soup and buns.

For a price, you too can clutch pearls at Pearl Market

🍴 LIQUN ROAST DUCK RESTAURANT 利群烤鸭店
Peking Duck YY

☎ 6702 5681, 6705 5578; 11 Beixiangfeng Hutong, 北翔凤胡同11号; ⏰ 10am-10pm; Ⓜ Qianmen

This restaurant is Beixiangfeng Hutong's pride. The service may be curt and the atmosphere frenetic, but the duck lives up to its stellar reputation. If you want to eat between 11am and 2.30pm or 5pm and 10pm, you'll need reservations. It takes about an hour to prepare and serve each bird.

⭐ PLAY

⭐ RED THEATRE 红剧场
Kung-Fu

☎ 6710 3671; 44 Xingfu Dajie, 幸福大街44号; tickets Y180-380; ⏰ 5.15pm & 7.30pm; Ⓜ Chongwenmen, then taxi

This theatre's long-running *The Legend of Kung-Fu* production depicts a boy's journey to kung-fu master. It's like a flashy Broadway musical except the story is propelled by thrilling kung-fu moves instead of song-and-dance numbers.

>SOUTH CHAOYANG 朝阳南

Chaoyang, south of Ritan Park, has a bit of a split personality. You can experience both the grit and crowds of local markets and the glitz, energy (and construction dust) of the Central Business Disrict (CBD).

The CBD sits northeast of Jianguomenwai Dajie and has wheelers-and-dealers yammering on their mobile phones over the roaring grind of cranes. Dozens of new offices and skyscrapers are being built here, including the spectacular new headquarters of China's national broadcaster (CCTV). This area also has terrific restaurants as well as fashionable lounges and bars such as Centro and Lan.

South Chaoyang is also a favourite with shoppers, who are drawn by the famous Panjiayuan Antique Market, the copycat goods at the Silk Market and upscale malls such as those in the shiny new LG Twin Towers.

The subway network is extremely limited in South Chaoyang. Taxi is the most efficient way to get around.

SOUTH CHAOYANG

DISTRICTS

SOUTH CHAOYANG

 # SEE

CCTV BUILDING 中央台大厦

Dongsanhuan Zhonglu, 东三环中路;
Guomao

Like a wonky cube with the centre punched out, CCTV's new 775ft headquarters towers over Chaoyang's central business district. The building, designed by Dutch firm OMA, isn't even finished yet but is already one of the most raved about new structures in town. The outside should be completed by Spring 2008. See also p17.

CREATION GALLERY 可创艺苑

☎ 8561 7570; www.creationgallery .com.cn; **Ritan Donglu,** 日坛东路;
🕙 **10am-7pm Tue-Sun;** **Yongli, then taxi**

Opened and curated by the son of celebrated landscape artist Li Keran (1907–89), this gallery specialises in contemporary works. It's a favourite place for travellers to scoop up prints, sculpture and oil paintings by up-and-coming artists from all over China.

RITAN PARK 日坛公园

☎ 6592 5576; **Ritan Lu,** 日坛路; **admission free;** 🕙 **6am-9pm;** **Yongli, then taxi**

Built in 1530, this lovely pine-filled park was where emperors came to make sacrifices to the sun. These days, the large ritual altar is used by kite flyers and taichi practitioners.

 # SHOP

BEIJING CURIO CITY
北京古玩城 *Market*

☎ 6774 7711; **21 Dongsanhuan Nanlu,** 东三环南路21号; 🕙 **9.30am-6.30pm;** **Guomao, then taxi**

This four-floor covered market is excellent for jewellery, carpets and Chinese curios. Vendors here are generally low key, leaving you time to look around before the high-energy haggling begins.

COTTAGE
草舍 *Homewares/Crafts*

☎ 8561 1517; **4 Ritan Beilu,** 日坛北路 4号; 🕙 **9.30am-7.30pm;** **Yongli, then taxi**

Selling antique-style furniture, small vases and homewares, this store is beautifully set up for browsing and the helpful staff are great for gift suggestions.

DONGJIAO SHICHANG
东郊市场 *Market*

Dongsanhuan Zhonglu, 东三环中路;
🕙 **10am-6pm;** **Guomao**

If you're after authentic local atmosphere, check out this ramshackle market. On weekends it's a sprawling collection of de-

COMMUNIST KITSCH

Mao memorabilia remains one of Beijing's most popular souvenirs and is sold everywhere there are tourists. Vendors say Mao's *Little Red Book*, a collection of his quotations, is still the number-one seller. But if that doesn't do it for you, head to the souvenir stalls at the exit of the Chairman Mao Memorial Hall (p39), where there is everything from Mao pocket watches to Mao-emblazoned lighters that play the Chinese national anthem.

manding crowds and messy stalls where everyone from vendors selling pet fish to old-fashioned cobblers set up. Several specialist buildings lurk at the back, including **Dongjiao Lushan Jiu Tea City** (东郊绿山九茶城; ☽ 8am-5pm), which is filled with stalls selling loose tea and tea sets.

🛍 **MUSHI** 模西 *Clothing*
☎ 5865 8927/8093; www.mushi.com
.cn; 1st fl, LG Twin Towers Shopping Mall
B-12, Jianguomenwai Dajie, 建国门
外大街乙12号LG双子座大厦1层;
☽ 10.30am-8pm Mon-Sat, 1-6pm Sun;
Ⓜ Yonganli
French-born Caroline Deleens lived in China as a teenager, studied fashion design in Paris and now mixes European styles with Chinese fabrics in her funky Mushi line.

🏛 **PANJIAYUAN ANTIQUE MARKET** 潘家园古玩市场
Antiques/Crafts/Collectables
☎ 6775 2405; Panjiayuan Lu, 潘家园路; ☽ 8.30am-6pm Mon-Fri, 4.30am-6.30pm Sat & Sun; Ⓜ Guomao, then taxi
Beijing's most beloved flea market sells almost every Chinese object imaginable. Bargain hard (vendors sometimes start at 10 times the going price) and treat any claims about 'antique objects' with scepticism. Not much goes on here during the week, but on weekends this is one of the most fun and dynamic places in Beijing. See also p22.

Ritan Park was formerly the scene of sacrifices

DISTRICTS

SOUTH CHAOYANG

☷ RITAN OFFICE BUILDING 日坛商务楼 Clothing

☎ 6502 1528; 15a Guanghua Lu, 光华路甲15号; ⏱ 10am-7pm; Ⓜ Yonganli
The office workers moved out and the hip clothing stores moved in. It's an odd set-up but the stores are great with wares a notch up from what you usually find in the markets. A favourite with nearby embassy staff.

☷ SILK MARKET 秀水市场 Market

☎ 6501 8811; Jianguomenwai Dajie, 建国门外大街; ⏱ 9am-9pm; Ⓜ Yonganli
So popular it's included on some bus tours, the Silk Market is a long-time favourite with visitors looking to pick up cheap (ie fake) 'brand name' clothing.

Silk Market

☷ ZHAOJIA CHAOWAI CLASSICAL FURNITURE MARKET 兆佳朝外古典家具市场 Market

☎ 6770 6402; Dongsanhuan Nanlu, 东三环路; ⏱ 10am-6pm Mon-Fri, 9am-6pm Sat & Sun; Ⓜ Guomao, then taxi
Traditional- and antique-style Chinese furniture and boxes pack this popular multifloor market. International shipping offices are on the 1st floor.

☷ EAT

☷ GRANDMA'S KITCHEN 祖母的厨房 Western
Y

☎ 6503 2893; 11 Xiushui Nanjie, 秀水南街11号; ⏱ 7.30am-11.30pm; Ⓜ Yonganli; Ⓥ
Authentic American classics, heaped portions and excellent waitstaff are the hallmarks of this cosy home-style restaurant. Families pack this place so there's always plenty of kids running among the tables. English menu available.

☷ JENNY LOU'S 婕鈮璐食品店 Deli
Y

☎ 8563 0626; 4 Ritan Beilu, 日坛北路4号; ⏱ 8am-10pm; Ⓜ Yonganli, then taxi; Ⓥ
This Western-oriented grocery store has it all – Lebanese yogurt, French cognac, Russian beer and snacks and foodstuff from back home, wherever that may be.

DISTRICTS

SOUTH CHAOYANG

MAKYE AME 玛吉阿米
Tibetan YY
☎ 6506 9616; www.makyeame.cn;
2nd fl, 11a Xiushui Nanjie, 秀水南
街甲11号2层; ⏱ 11.30am-2am;
Ⓜ Yonganli

This atmospheric Tibetan restaurant has the best of everything: welcoming staff, traditional decorations and all the classics including yak meat, *momo* (Tibetan dumplings) and yogurt. Dinner reservations are recommended on Friday and Saturday.

SCHINDLER'S TANKSTELLE
申德勒加油站 *European* YY
☎ 8562 6439; 15 Guanghua Lu, 光华路
15号; ⏱ 10am-midnight; Ⓜ Jianguomen;
Ⓥ

Authentic German atmosphere and classics like pork rump and apple strudel make this a great choice when you're in the Ritan Park area. Small glasses of terrific draught beer start at Y28. English menu available.

XIAO WANG'S FAMILY RESTAURANT 小王府
Chinese Homestyle YY
☎ 6591 3255; 2 Guanghua Dongli, 光
华路东里2号; ⏱ 11am-10.30pm;
Ⓜ Guomao

Xiao Wang serves up some of the city's best comfort food including deep-fried spare ribs and hot-and-spicy Xinjiang chicken wings.

A long-time favourite with both locals and travellers. English menu available.

XIHEYAJU RESTAURANT
羲和雅居餐厅 *Sichuan* YY
☎ 8561 7643; Ritan Park, 日坛公园;
⏱ 11am-2pm & 5-10pm; Ⓜ Yonganli, then taxi

Hotpot and pork ribs are among Xiheyaju's excellent Sichuan dishes. Set in a leafy corner of Ritan Park, this restaurant has a dining room, an outdoor patio and a stunning glassed-in conservatory.

DRINK

CENTRO 炫酷 *Lounge*
☎ 6561 8833, ext 6388; Kerry Center Hotel, 1 Guanghua Lu, 光华路1号, 嘉

Sun 'Simon' Shuo
Head bartender, Centro (p77)

What are Beijingers' favourite drinks these days? It's changing, but most Chinese business people still don't like cocktails; they'll go for a nice aged wine or single malt scotch. Local beer is the most popular for young people. **You work in a bar all day, where do you go out to relax?** Out to more bars! I don't care about the music so much. I just like to hang out and talk to the bartenders. **Where's the best place to go to sample Beijing's nightlife?** There's so much and it's changing all the time. Things can be here one day, gone the next. People should check out *That's Beijing* and magazines like that to find out what's going on. **Where should visitors head for a taste of the 'real' Beijing?** Forget the Peking duck and ditch the tourist map. Just pick a neighbourhood, walk around and relax in the local way.

里中心饭店; ⏰ 24hr; Ⓜ **Guomao**
Hot jazz, cool colourful décor
and the best martinis around.
The place of choice for business
people to wheel and deal or just
impress the hell out of their dates.

Ⓨ LAN 兰会所 *Lounge/Club*
☎ 5109 6012; 4th fl, LG Twin Towers
Shopping Mall B-12, Jianguomenwai
Dajie, 建国门外大街乙12号双子座
大厦4层; ⏰ 10am-3am; Ⓜ Yonganli
As if live jazz, an oyster bar, a cigar
lounge and a monster wine list
weren't enough, Lan had celebrity
designer Philippe Starck do the
one-of-a-kind interior, making this
club the nightcrawl destination of
the hour.

Ⓨ STONE BOAT BAR
石舫酒吧 *Bar*
☎ 6501 9986; Ritan Park, 日坛公园南
门内; ⏰ 10am-late; Ⓜ Jianguomen

Set up in a real-life stone boat on
one of Ritan Park's large ponds,
this low-key bar serves all the
standard cocktails, spirits, beers
and café-style food. To enter after
the park closes, just tell the guards
at the south gate where you're
going and they'll let you in.

PLAY

☆ BANANA 吧那那 *Club*
☎ 6526 3939; SciTech Hotel, 22
Jianguomenwai Dajie, 建国门外大街
22号赛特饭店; cover charge Y20-30;
⏰ 8.30pm-4am Sun-Thu, 8.30pm-5am
Fri & Sat; Ⓜ Jianguomen or Yonganli
This club may not look like much
on the outside, but inside you'll
get an explosion of colour and
music that runs from chill-out to
techno. There's a massive dance
floor downstairs; the upstairs
lounge is where guest DJs play.

>HAIDIAN 海淀

Whether you're looking to roam imperial parks or want to experience some of Beijing's best nightlife, Haidian gives you more options than you'll know what to do with.

The historic Summer Palace is the jewel of the district, but Haidian is also home to some of the most expansive and unique green spaces in the entire city. The Old Summer Palace Park and Fragrant Hills Park, once the exclusive stomping grounds of Chinese royalty, are both standouts.

Haidian is also home to heaps of post-secondary institutions, including Peking University and Qinghua University, two of the country's most prestigious schools. The district's huge student population drives an exciting club scene, now concentrated near the Wudaokou light-rail stop and along Chengfu Lu.

There's one light rail line that swoops up towards northern Haidian, but the distances between the district's sights are generally enormous. For the most part, you'll need to rely on taxis to get around.

HAIDIAN

👁 SEE
Great Bell Temple............1 B4
Old Summer Palace
  Park.............................2 A1
Wuta Temple Park.........3 B6

🍴 EAT
Isshin 4 B2

⭐ PLAY
13 CLUB 5 A2
D-2.................................6 A2
Lush...............................7 B2
Propaganda...................8 B3

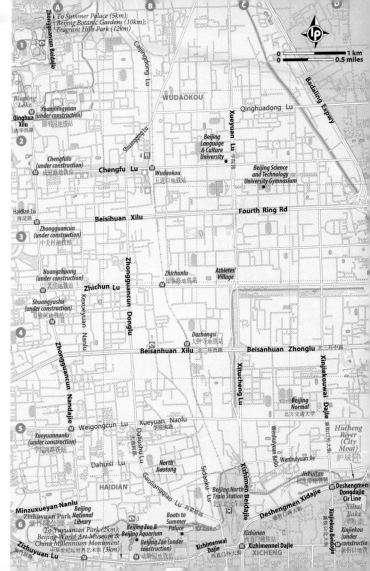

A **B** **C** **D**

0 _____ 1 km
0 _____ 0.5 miles

To Summer Palace (5km);
Beijing Botanic Gardens (10km);
Fragrant Hills Park (12km)

Zhonghua Beidajie

Cuiqingdong Lu

WUDAOKOU

Blessing Lake

Yuanmingyuan
(under construction)
圆明园地铁站

Qinghua Xilu
清华西路

Shuangqing Lu

Qinghuadong Lu

Xueyuan Lu 学院路

Beijing Language & Culture University

Badaling Expwy

Chengfulu
(under construction)
成府路地铁站

Chengfu Lu

Wudaokou
五道口地铁站

Beijing Science and Technology University Gymnasium

Haidian Lu
海淀路

Beisihuan Xilu

Fourth Ring Rd

Zhongguancun
(under construction)
中关村地铁站

Huangzhuang
(under construction)
黄庄地铁站

Zhongguancun Donglu

Zhichunlu
知春路地铁站

Zhichun Lu

Athletes' Village

Shuangyushu
(under construction)
双榆树地铁站

Kexueyuan Nanlu

Xitucheng Lu

Beisanhuan Xilu 北三环西路

Dazhongsi
大钟寺一站地铁站

Beisanhuan Zhonglu 北三环路

Xinjiekouwai Dajie

Beijing Normal
北方交通大学

Zhongguancun Nandajie

Weigongcun Lu

Xueyuan Nanlu
学院南路

Dahuishu Lu

Hucheng River (City Moat)
护城河

Xueyuannanlu
(under construction)
学院南路地铁站

Wenhuatuan Beilu

Wenhuatuan Jie

Dahuisi Lu

HAIDIAN

Gaoliangqiao Lu

Sidaoku Lu

North Jiaotong

Jishuitan
积水潭地铁站

Deshengmen Dongdajie
Cir Line

Xihai Lake

Xinjiekou Beidajie

Minzuxueyan Nanlu
紫竹院公园

Zizhuyuan Park

Beijing National Library

Beijing World Art Museum &
China Millennium Monument (3km)

To Yuyuantan Park (2km);

Zizhuyuan Lu

Beijing Zoo &
Beijing Aquarium

Boats to Summer Palace

Beijing Zoo (under construction)
动物园地铁站

Deshengmen Xidajie

Xizhimen Beidajie

Xizhimennei Dajie

Xizhimen
西直门地铁站

Xizhimenwai Dajie

Xizhimen

Xinjiekou (under construction)
新街口地铁站

XICHENG

SEE

BEIJING BOTANIC GARDENS
北京植物园
☎ 6259 1283; Wofusi Lu, 卧佛寺路; admission Y5; ⏰ 6am-9pm 1 May-31 Oct, last entry 7pm, 7am-7pm 1 Nov-31 Apr, last entry 5pm; Ⓜ Gucheng, exit D, then taxi

These gardens have terrific walks and heaps of things to visit including a Conservatory (entry is Y50) and the Sleeping Buddha Temple (Y5).

BEIJING WORLD ART MUSEUM & CHINA MILLENNIUM MONUMENT
中华世纪坛世界艺术馆
☎ 6852 7108; www.worldartmuseum .com; Yuyuantan Nanlu, 玉渊潭南路; adult/senior & student Y30/20; ⏰ 9am-6pm, last entry 5pm; Ⓜ Junshibowu-guan-Military Museum

Housed in the China Millennium Monument, the World Art Museum hosts killer temporary exhibitions ranging from Inca sculpture to avant-garde photography. The Millennium Monument is shaped like a giant sundial and you can climb up its face for views of Beijing.

FRAGRANT HILLS PARK
香山公园
☎ 6259 1283; northwest Beijing, 北京西北; admission Y10, temples Y10; ⏰ 6am-6.30pm 1 Apr-30 Jun & 1 Sep-15 Nov, 6am-7pm 1 Jul-31 Aug, 6am-6pm 16 Nov-31 Mar; Ⓜ Gucheng, exit D, then taxi

Snuggled in the hills, this park is a favourite with hikers and walkers. Stunning temples dot the grounds (English signs point the way) and on nonpolluted days, the views from Incense-Burner Peak are unforgettable. Sights close at 5pm.

GREAT BELL TEMPLE 大钟寺
☎ 6225 1843; 31a Beisanhuan Xilu, 北三环西路甲31号; adult/child Y10/4; ⏰ 8.30am-4.30pm; Ⓜ Dazhongsi

Are bells the most important thing that ever happened to China? Probably not. But this museum does such a bang-up job explaining these instruments it makes you wonder whether bells should be right up there with inventing paper and gun powder. An audio guide is Y10, with a Y100 deposit.

OLD SUMMER PALACE PARK 圆明园
☎ 6262 8501; www.yuanmingyuan park.com.cn in Chinese; 28 Qinghua Xilu, 清华西路28号; admission to ruins Y15, park Y10; ⏰ 7am-7pm May-Aug, 7am-6.30pm Sep & Oct & Jan-Mar, 7am-5.30pm Nov & Dec; Ⓜ Wudaokou, then taxi

Not to be confused with the Summer Palace (opposite), 5km north, the Old Summer Palace is where Emperor Qianlong (1711–99)

WORTH THE TRIP: SUMMER PALACE 颐和园

The **Summer Palace** (☎ 6288 1144; www.summerpalace-china.com; Yiheyuan Lu, 颐和园路; admission 1 Apr-31 Oct Y60, 1 Nov-31 Mar Y50; ☷ 9am-5pm 1 Apr-31 Oct, last entry 4.30pm, 9am-4pm 1 Nov-31 Mar, last entry 3.30pm; ☉ Wudaokou, then taxi) is the pleasure palace of Emperor Qianlong (1711–99); see p15.

Just inside the East Gate is the chief palace structure, the **Hall of Benevolence & Longevity**, where the emperor handled state affairs and received envoys.

Nearby, the **Garden of Virtue & Harmony** comprises two halls and a theatre stage. The stage is where the imperial family watched Peking opera, a favourite of Empress Cixi. From May through August it hosts free performances (usually acrobatics or traditional dance) hourly, 9am to 4pm. Theatrical costumes and props are displayed in the neighbouring pavilions.

The **Long Corridor**, a 728m pavilion decorated with mythical scenes, is west of here. **Longevity Hill** looms to the north and has most of the palace's grand halls and temples. Further on is Cixi's infamous **marble boat** (see p84), and the ferry (Y8) that crosses to South Lake Island.

South Lake Island's **Hall of Embracing the Universe** contains a small exhibition on Puyi, the last emperor. Go south to the **Western Corridor** (see p15) or north to **Wenchang Gallery**.

To get to the palace by boat, see p147. Admission to the grounds only is Y30 cheaper and they're open extended hours. An audioguide is Y40, with a Y100 deposit.

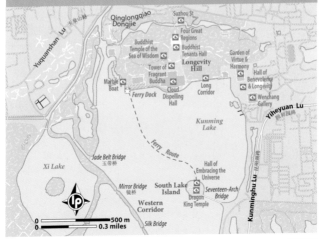

Old Summer Palace: skateboarding frowned upon

WUTA TEMPLE 五塔寺

☎ 6217 3543; 24 Wutasi Cun, 五塔
寺村24号; admission to temple Y5,
museum Y15; ⏰ 9am-4pm Tue-Sun;
🚇 Xizhimen, then taxi

If you can squeeze yourself up
the doll-sized staircase, you'll get
an up-close look at this Buddhist
temple's unique five-pagoda
roof. Once you've squeezed back
down the staircase, check out the
interesting Stone Carving Museum at the back of the temple
grounds.

YUYUANTAN PARK
玉渊潭公园

☎ 6256 5886; Yuyuantan Nanlu, 玉渊
潭南路; adult/child Y2/1; ⏰ 6am-
10pm, last entry 9pm; 🚇 Junshibowu-
guan-Military Museum

With a huge body of water divided
into east and west lakes; this is a
lovely park for long walks. If your
time's limited, go for the prettier
west lake route.

had Jesuit missionaries design a
Western-style palace with all the
trimmings. Unfortunately, foreign
soldiers pummelled it to pieces
during the Second Opium War.
Now you can crawl among the
'ruins', peruse the before-and-after
photos and wander the enormous
grounds. Last entry is one hour
before closing.

MYSTERY OF THE MARBLE BOAT

Did Empress Cixi, the de-facto last ruler of Imperial China, really squander her navy's money
on the Summer Palace's marble boat (p83)? Turns out, this and much of what's held true
about this ruler, who is blamed for everything from palace murders to wanton squandering of
the imperial fortune, may be bunk. As more historians have access to China, many are ques-
tioning what we think we know about Cixi, discovering, for example, that the marble boat,
long held as a symbol of her excess, was built before she was even born. Sterling Seagrave's
Dragon Lady is the best book on the subject and builds a convincing case that bad translations
and shoddy journalism in Qing-era China carried myth to the masses as fact.

EAT

ISSHIN 日本料理一心
North Asian   *YY*
☎ 8261 0136; www.isshin.info in
Chinese; 35 Chengfu Lu, 成府路35号;
11am-2pm & 5-10pm Sun-Thu, 5-11pm Fri
& Sat; ⊖ Wudaokou

Japanese expatriates give this
restaurant's hotpot and luxury
sashimi plates the stamp of approval. Service is reserved but
goes with the coldly modern
dark décor. The entrance is off
Shuangqing Lu (双清路) north of
Chengfu Lu. Turn left through the
big metal arch.

PLAY

☆ 13 CLUB 13 俱乐部
Live Music
☎ 8261 9213; 161 Chengfu Lu, 成府
路161号; ⊙ 6pm-late; ⊖ Wudaokou,
then taxi

Local punk and metal bands are
Club 13's bread and butter, but
the laid-back musician-managers
are open to anything. Even left-
field choices like Mongolian folk
music make the program.

☆ D-22 酒吧 *Live Music/Films*
☎ 6265 3177; www.d22beijing
.com; 242 Chengfu Lu, 成府路242号;
⊙ 6pm-2am; ⊖ Wudaokou, then taxi

A hub for student filmmakers and
musicians, D-22 lets bands doing
everything from jazz to rock to
'experimental' music plug into their
awesome sound system. Movies
(foreign or Chinese) are screened at
7pm on Wednesday and Thursday.

☆ LUSH *Live Music/Films*
☎ 8286 3566; www.lushbeijing.com;
2nd fl, 1 Huaqing Jiayuan, Chengfu Lu, 成
府路花清嘉园1号楼2层; ⊙ 24hr;
⊖ Wudaokou

Whether they're quaffing coffee
or slamming down beers, Chinese
and foreign students camp out
here around the clock. There are
movies on Monday and live bands
on Friday. Open-mike night on
Sunday is standing room only.

☆ PROPAGANDA *Club*
East gate, Huaqing Jiayuan, 花清嘉园
东门; ⊙ 8pm-late; ⊖ Wudaokou

Loved for its meat-market reputation as much as for its hip-hop
soundtrack, this club is a long-time
student favourite and is packed
with dancers on weekends.

>XICHENG 西城

Packed chock-a-block with sights, restaurants and nightlife, Xicheng is one of the most engrossing districts in Beijing. Beihai Park, once part of the Forbidden City, has beautiful scenery and is always animated by local exercisers. Elsewhere, Xicheng is home to several new additions to the city's skyline, including the Capital Museum and the controversial National Grand Theatre.

But for most Beijingers, Xicheng is known for the wonderful Sichahai area, one of the city's social hubs. Called 'Houhai' by locals, the area surrounds three lakes (Xihai, Houhai and Qianhai), whose shores are packed with restaurants, nightlife and shopping. Older folks come here to relax by the lakes or practise ballroom dancing at the Di'anmen Xidajie entrance. Young people come to hit the trendy bars and to make out on the benches. There are also some excellent *hutong* (traditional alleyway) areas surrounding the lakes.

For shoppers, Houhai's Yandai Xiejie is good for clothes and trinkets.

XICHENG

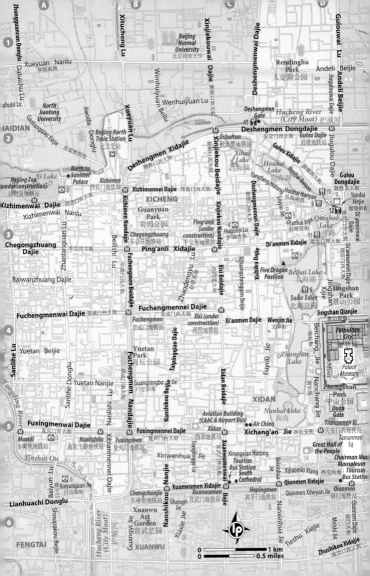

SEE

BEIHAI PARK 北海公园

☎ 6403 1102; Wenjin Jie, 文津街; admission Y10; ☉ 6.30am-8pm, sights 9am-5pm, last entry 4pm; ☉ Tiananmen Xi, then taxi

Beihai's one of those parks that really does have something for everyone. If you're after culture, there are fantastic temples and pavilions to explore (tickets are usually an extra Y5; Yong'an Temple is Y20 including park admission). If you're after recreation, you can hit the walking paths, take a paddle boat on the lake or crash someone's *qi gong* session.

BEIJING EXHIBITION HALL 北京展览馆

Xizhimenwai Dajie, 西直门外大街; ☉ Xizhimen

Opened in 1954 to mark the fifth anniversary of the founding of the People's Republic of China, this hall is a monstrous cousin to Stalin's notorious 'seven sisters' buildings that dot the Moscow skyline. It now hosts trade and professional conventions.

CAPITAL MUSEUM 首都博物馆

☎ 6337 0491; www.capitalmuseum.org .cn; 16 Fuxingmenwai Dajie, 复兴门外大街16号; admission Y30; ☉ 9am-5pm Tue-Sun, last entry 4pm; ☉ Muxidi

The mysteriously named White Cloud Temple is enveloped in white cloud

Opened in 2006 to the dropped jaws of jaded culture vultures, this museum has raised the bar for every cultural institution in town. Exhibits brilliantly showcase major Chinese cultural achievements from Buddha statues and porcelain to the founding of Beijing itself. The presentation is flawless and the exquisitely designed building (see p17) beautifully sets off the collections. An audio guide is Y30 with a Y100 deposit.

MEI LANFANG FORMER RESIDENCE 梅兰芳纪念馆
☎ 6618 3598; www.meilanfang.com.cn; 9 Huguosi Lu, 护国寺路9号; admission Y10; ☼ 9am-4pm Tue-Sun Apr-Nov; ◉ Jishuitan, then taxi
Peking opera icon Mei Lanfang (1894–1961) was famous for interpreting female roles as well as for popularising Peking opera (p20) in the West. This little courtyard museum shows off his costumes and photos. English captions throughout.

PRINCE GONG'S RESIDENCE 恭王府
☎ 6616 5005; 14 Liuyin Jie, 柳荫街 14号; adult/child Y20/10; ☼ 8am-6pm; ◉ Gulou Dajie, then taxi
Elaborate gardens and elegant rockeries are the standouts at this compound, once belonging

to Prince Gong, a Qing official famous for his statesmanship during the Second Opium War. From May to October, there are **Peking opera** (☎ 6618 6628; tickets Y80-120; ☼ 7.30-8.40pm) performances too.

WHITE CLOUD TEMPLE 白云观
☎ 6618 2739; www.taoist.org.cn; Baiyunguan Jie, 白云观街; admission Y10; 8.30am-4.30pm May-Sep, 8.30am-4pm Oct-Apr; ◉ Nanlishilu
Taoist monks with their signature topknots and unique dress tend to this vast temple complex, home of the Chinese Taoist Association. The Spring Festival (p26) temple fair here is one of the city's best.

SHOP

MU HANDCRAFTS 穆手工

Souvenirs
☎ 8402 1831; www.craftxm.com in Chinese; 11 Yandai Xiejie, 烟袋斜街 11号; ☼ 10am-midnight; ◉ Gulou Dajie
The shelves here are stocked with artisan paper and hide-bound notebooks all made by hand. Some come with plain designs, others are emblazoned with Peking opera masks or typical Beijing scenes.

Ao Jun
Senior chef, Fangshan Restaurant (opposite)

Why did you get interested in doing imperial cuisine? Because you're always dealing with high quality ingredients and you must always do your work very well. There's also a repertoire of more than 1000 dishes from the Manchu and Han imperial courts, so that's exciting for a chef. **What do you like cooking when you're not working?** Any kind of family-style seafood dish with vegetables in season. It's delicious and has lots of nutrition. **Any famous Beijing street food you'd recommend?** I like *xiao wo tou* (小窝头, steamed corn bun) and anything with beans like *yun dou juan* (芸豆卷, mashed bean roll). **What do you do for fun when you're not working?** Besides eating? For rest, I like doing day trips to the countryside. For culture, I still like the Forbidden City.

EAT

FANGSHAN RESTAURANT
仿膳饭庄 *Imperial*　　　YYY
☎ 6401 1889; www.fangshan
fanzhuang.com.cn in Chinese; Jade
Islet, Beihai Park, 北海公园琼岛;
🕑 11.30am-2.30pm & 5.30-10.30pm;
🚇 Tiananmen Xi, then taxi

You'll be blinded by the gold-and-red décor but this is a kitchily fun place nonetheless. The multi-course menus are all based on the imperial court's favourite dishes. English menu available.

NO NAME RESTAURANT 无
名 *Regional Chinese*　　　YY
☎ 6618 6061; 1 Dajinsi Hutong, 大金丝
胡同1号; 🕑 11am-midnight; 🚇 Gulou
Dajie, then taxi

Curious about Yunnan cuisine? This stylish but relaxed restaurant is a great place to start. It not only

BEIJING'S LATEST ART TREND...FOOD
Artists are opening restaurants in Beijing almost as fast as they're selling paintings. Yuelu Shanwu (right) is one of several restaurants owned by cynical realist painter Fang Lijun. Over in North Chaoyang, three struggling Guizhou artists opened Three Guizhou Men (p60) to pay the bills. It's so successful they now use it to display their work.

has a picture of each dish on the English menu, but also an entry explaining the flavours and spices used – we recommend the *dai* fish and Yunnan rice noodles. The bubbling fountain and helpful waitstaff add to the enjoyable atmosphere.

NUAGE 庆云楼
Southeast Asian　　　YY
☎ 6401 9581; www.nuage.com.cn;
22 Qianhai Dongyan, 前海东沿22号;
🕑 11am-2pm & 5-9.45pm; 🚇 Gulou
Dajie, then taxi

Slick décor, slightly snobby staff and beautifully presented Viet-namese food make for a memorable meal. There's a lovely lakeside view and a fantastic variety of lemongrass dishes and *pho* soups. English menu available.

YUELU SHANWU 岳麓山屋
Regional Chinese　　　YY
☎ 6617 2696; 19a Qianhai Xiyan, 前
海西沿甲19号; 🕑 11am-11pm;
🚇 Gulou Dajie, then taxi

The catalogue-sized English picture menu is heavy on spicy, smoked and garlic-packed dishes, inspired by the cuisine of Hunan province. Tuck into popular dishes like stir-fried radish with dried pork or fish and chilli and watch the boats bob by on Qianhai Lake.

DISTRICTS

XICHENG

DRINK

NO NAME BAR 白枫 Bar
☎ 6401 8541; 3 Qianhai Dongyan, 前海东沿3号; noon-2am; Ⓜ Gulou Dajie
The success of this laid-back watering hole is what got the original Houhai bar scene going. Sitting on the banks of Qianhai Lake, it's still considered by many to be the best bar of the bunch.

WEST WING 西厢房 Bar
☎ 8208 2836; inside Deshengmen Gate, 德胜门内; Ⓜ 2pm-2am; Ⓜ Jishuitan
Inside an old watchtower north of Houhai, this bar caters to a lesbian clientele. Relax with a drink near the first-floor bar or head downstairs where there's darts, sofas and the ever-popular punching bag.

PLAY

NATIONAL GRAND THEATRE 国家大剧院 Theatre
☎ 6606 4705; www.national grandtheater.com; west of Great Hall of the People, 人民大会堂西侧; Ⓜ Tiananmen Xi
One of the jewels in Beijing's architectural crown (see also p17), this colossal venue contains an opera house, a concert hall and a theatre. By the time you're in town, everything from Peking opera and Chinese folk music to modern dance troupes to visiting symphonies will be staged

West Wing

here. Check the website for the schedule.

★ SANWEI BOOKSTORE 三味
书屋 *Live Music/Peking Opera*
☎ 6601 3204; 60 Fuxingmennei Dajie,
复兴门内大街60号; ◷ 10am-10pm;
◉ Xidan

This cool little bookstore has a 2nd-floor teahouse that often hosts jazz gigs or Peking opera in the evening. Call ahead or drop by for the performance schedule and ticket prices.

★ WHAT? BAR 什么?酒吧
Live Music
72 Beichang Jie, 北长街72号; ◷ 3pm-midnight; ◉ Tiananmen Xi, then taxi

With its eclectic regulars, this tiny club is one of best places to hang out in Beijing. Everyone from blues musicians to local goth rockers have played What?'s shoebox-sized stage. The Y30 Friday and Saturday night cover charge includes a complimentary beer.

>XUANWU 宣武

Xuanwu is a charming district southwest of the Forbidden City with traditional *hutong* (alleyway) neighbourhoods, shopping and lots of venues staging traditional Chinese entertainment like Peking opera and acrobatics.

Xuanwu's popular pedestrian shopping streets are in the district's northeast. Liulichang Xijie and Liulichang shops specialise in antique-style curios, art and calligraphy materials, while on Dazhalan Jie restaurants and shops over 100 years old rub shoulders with trendy clothing stores blaring Chinese pop music.

Further south, Beijing's Muslim Quarter is home to a large community of Hui (Chinese Muslims) as well as Fayuan Temple, an important Buddhist temple.

At the time of research, the far-eastern end of Dazhalan Jie, the nearby *hutong* and Qianmen Dajie were sealed off for massive renovations and slated to reopen as an 'old-style' pedestrian shopping area in time for the Olympics.

XUANWU

◉ SEE
Fayuan Temple 1 B4
Grand View Garden 2 A5
Niujie Mosque 3 B3

🏠 SHOP
Neiliansheng Shoes 4 D2

Xinghai Yuehaixuan
  Musical Instruments ... 5 C2

🍴 EAT
Fengzeyuan 6 D3
Turpan Restaurant 7 B3

⭐ PLAY
Huguang Guild
  Hall 8 C3
Lao She Teahouse 9 D2
Liyuan Theatre 10 C3
Tianqiao Acrobatics
  Theatre 11 D4

DISTRICTS

XUANWU

SEE
FAYUAN TEMPLE 法源寺

☎ 6353 3966; 7 Fayuansi Qianjie, 法源寺前街7号; admission Y5; ⏰ 8.30am-4pm; Ⓜ Changchunjie, then taxi
Home to the China Buddhism College, this temple was established in the 7th century and buzzes with worshippers and student monks. At the time of research its striking Buddha effigies and pavilions were under wraps for pre-Olympic renovation but the tarps should be off by the time you read this.

GRAND VIEW GARDEN
大观园公园

☎ 6354 4993; 12 Nancaiyuan Jie, 南菜园街12号; admission Y40; ⏰ 8.30am-5.30pm, last entry 4.30pm; Ⓜ Changchunjie, then taxi
Built to replicate the garden described in Cao Xueqin's classic Chinese novel *Dream of the Red Mansion*, Grand View Garden is a stunner. Cryptic English signs mark the location of key story events. Signs and tourist maps sometimes label this park 'Beijing Museum of Red Chamber Culture and Art'.

NIUJIE MOSQUE
牛街礼拜寺

☎ 6353 2564; 88 Niu Jie, 牛街88号; admission Y10, Muslims free; ⏰ 8am-sunset; Ⓜ Changchunjie, then taxi
Dating back to the 10th century, this friendly mosque is a fascinating mix of Islamic and Chinese architectural styles. Dress appropriately (no shorts, bare shoulders or short skirts) and skip Friday during services.

SHOP
NEILIANSHENG SHOES
内联升鞋店 Shoes

☎ 6301 4863; 34 Dazhalan Jie, 大栅栏街34号; ⏰ 9am-9pm; Ⓜ Qianmen

MUSLIM QUARTER

There are 240,000 Hui and 70 mosques throughout greater Beijing, but the Niu Jie (Cow St) area, with its Muslim schools, restaurants, shops and the biggest mosque in the city (see Niujie Mosque, above), remains the community's hub.

Apartments striped with green (a symbolic colour in Islam) add to the area's Muslim character. Local residents were moved into these buildings when the government knocked down neighbourhood courtyard houses to widen Niu Jie, which was once just a narrow lane.

In the Muslim Quarter it's also worth checking out the north side of Nanheng Xijie (南横西街) and the surviving *hutong* network behind the mosque.

Islam meets China at Niujie Mosque

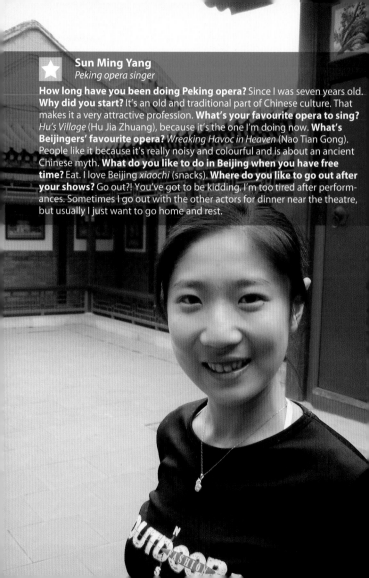

Sun Ming Yang
Peking opera singer

How long have you been doing Peking opera? Since I was seven years old. **Why did you start?** It's an old and traditional part of Chinese culture. That makes it a very attractive profession. **What's your favourite opera to sing?** *Hu's Village* (Hu Jia Zhuang), because it's the one I'm doing now. **What's Beijingers' favourite opera?** *Wreaking Havoc in Heaven* (Nao Tian Gong). People like it because it's really noisy and colourful and is about an ancient Chinese myth. **What do you like to do in Beijing when you have free time?** Eat. I love Beijing *xiaochi* (snacks). **Where do you like to go out after your shows?** Go out?! You've got to be kidding. I'm too tired after performances. Sometimes I go out with the other actors for dinner near the theatre, but usually I just want to go home and rest.

In business since 1853, Neiliansheng Shoes is famous for its handmade cloth shoes and once even supplied Deng Xiaoping. 'Foreigner sizes' (ie big) are often available.

🎸 XINGHAI YUEHAIXUAN MUSICAL INSTRUMENTS
星海乐海轩乐器 *Souvenirs*

☎ 6303 1472; 97 Liulichang Dongjie, 琉璃厂东街97号; ⏰ 9am-6.30pm; Ⓜ Hepingmen

Traditional Chinese instruments (souvenir to professional quality) are sold in this shop. Knowledgeable (albeit pushy) staff happily answer all questions.

🍴 EAT

🍴 FENGZEYUAN 丰泽园
Regional Chinese   YY

☎ 6318 6688; 83 Zhushikou Xidajie, 珠市口西大街83号; ⏰ 11am-2pm & 5-9pm; Ⓜ Qianmen, then taxi

Sea cucumber with scallion is among the hallmark dishes of this Beijing institution, which specialises in the light flavours and seafood dishes of Shandong cuisine.

🍴 TURPAN RESTAURANT 吐鲁番餐厅 *Muslim*   Y

☎ 8316 4691; 6 Niu Jie, 牛街6号; ⏰ 11am-2pm & 5-9pm; Ⓜ Xuanwumen, then taxi

Despite the starkly lit, cavernous dining rooms, many consider this to be the best Muslim restaurant on Niu Jie. The menu features dishes from all Muslim regions of China, including the ever-popular Xinjiang lamb kebabs (羊肉串).

⭐ PLAY

⭐ HUGUANG GUILD HALL
湖广会馆 *Peking Opera*

☎ 6351 8284; www.beijinghuguang.com; 3 Hufang Lu, 虎坊路3号; tickets Y150-580; ⏰ 7.30-8.35pm; Ⓜ Hepingmen, then taxi

Built in 1807, this guildhall affords one of the most enjoyable Peking opera (p20) experiences in town. Mei Lanfang (see p89) himself once performed here. Earphones are available (Y30) to translate performances into English or Japanese.

⭐ LAO SHE TEAHOUSE 老舍茶馆 *Peking Opera/Live Music*

☎ 6303 6830; www.laosheteahouse.com in Chinese; 3 Qianmen Xidajie, 前门西大街3号; ⏰ 10.30am-1am; Ⓜ Qianmen

The 3rd-floor theatre has nightly shows running from 7.50pm to 9.20pm (tickets Y60 to Y180), usually Peking opera (p20), Chinese folk music or Sichuan opera. Across the hall, the teahouse often has 20-minute afternoon folk music or shadow-puppet performances on the hour.

⭐ LIYUAN THEATRE 梨园剧场
Peking Opera
☎ 6301 6688, ext 8822; Jianguo Hotel Qianmen, 175 Yong'an Lu, 永安路 175号前门建国饭店; **tickets Y80-280;** ⏰ **7.30pm;** Ⓜ **Hepingmen, then taxi**
This theatre, off a hotel lobby, hosts slick Peking opera performances accompanied by English, French and Japanese subtitles.

⭐ TIANQIAO ACROBATICS THEATRE 天桥杂技剧场
Acrobatics
☎ **6303 7449; 95 Tianqiao Shichang Lu,** 天桥市场路95号; **tickets Y100-200;** ⏰ **7.15pm;** Ⓜ **Qianmen, then taxi**
Terrific acrobatics shows are staged at this theatre, but note that Tianqiao Theatre, which hosts domestic and foreign dance companies and singers, is across from here on Beiwei Lu – taxi drivers sometimes get them mixed up.

Detail of the Water Cube and the Bird's Nest (p103)

THE OLYMPICS

THE OLYMPICS

The 2008 Olympic Games are more than just an athletic event for China; they're a unique chance for the nation to show off its economic success and political heft on the international stage.

Historically, China's relationship with the Olympics was tumultuous, including complete boycotts of the Games from 1949 to 1980 when Taiwan was permitted to participate as the 'Republic of China'.

These days, however, local enthusiasm for the Games is palpable and it's hard to find a Beijinger who isn't counting the seconds until the opening ceremonies.

When the call went out for 70,000 Olympic and 30,000 Paralympic volunteers, the Beijing Organizing Committee was flooded with over 550,000 applications from eager locals.

Cao Zuozheng, a 103-year-old Beijinger, was so excited about the Games she applied to become an Olympic torchbearer. Despite the grandmother's training regime (which involved lugging a pretend torch along on 300m walks every day since 2004), organisers rejected the application citing her frailty. Cao's family is so worried about what the disappointment would do to her, they still haven't told her the news.

HISTORY

The first modern Olympic Games were held in 1896, the brainchild of Pierre de Coubertin, a Frenchman who believed sport could foster goodwill between nations. Beijing first set its sight on hosting the 2000 Games but lost to Sydney. When China was awarded the 2008 Olympics on 13 July 2001 the whole country erupted with excitement.

MASCOT MADNESS

Beijing's five Olympic mascots (collectively known as fuwa) are the breakout stars of the 2008 Games. Despite a police crackdown, the fuwa are so wildly popular, some counterfeiters have ditched their trade in fake Louis Vuitton to crank out low-quality versions of these cartoon-like characters.

Each fuwa symbolises one of the Olympic rings and one of the five traditional elements: Beibei represents water, Jingjing metal, Huanhuan fire, Yingying earth and Nini wood. When the first syllables of each mascot are joined together, you get Bejiing huanying ni or 'Beijing welcomes you'.

Beijing is spending an estimated US$40 billion on Olympic preparations including new venues, infrastructure, subway lines and a new international airport wing. Designed by British firm Foster + Partners, Terminal 3 is expected to handle 1400 flights per day during the Games. Built according to feng shui guidelines, the terminal will be illuminated with red and yellow lights at night to enhance what's described as the building's 'dragon-like' appearance.

The city has had minimal success tackling environmental issues, and air pollution is considered by many to be the biggest menace to a successful Games. The relocation of an estimated 1.5 million Beijingers to make way for new roads and modern buildings has also caused controversy.

BEIJING VENUES

As many as 31 venues around Beijing are earmarked to host Olympic events. Sporting venues and gymnasiums all over the city are being renovated and revamped. Test events began in 2007 and most sporting associations gave the buildings positive reviews.

Most events will be held in Beijing, though a handful of events will take place in other Chinese cities. Tianjin, Shanghai, Shenyan and Qinhuangdao will host some of the football (soccer) preliminaries, Qingdao will host sailing races and Hong Kong has taken charge of equestrian events.

The stars of the Olympic skyline are the built-from-scratch National Stadium and National Aquatics Centre. The stadium, which will host most track-and-field events, as well as opening and closing ceremonies, is known as the Bird's Nest because of its exposed criss-cross supports around a hollow centre. Nearby, the aquatics centre, which will host most swimming and diving events, has been christened the Water Cube for its blue exterior pocked with bubbles. The Water Cube's yin balances the stadium's yang in architectural feng shui. Both buildings are spectacular and more than live up to the hype. There's been talk of opening them for public visits well before the Olympics kicks off, but nothing was confirmed at the time of writing. For more details on the architecture, see p17.

OLYMPICS PRACTICALITIES

The 2008 Games run from 8 August to 24 August. As the number 8 *(ba)* is considered lucky in Chinese (it rhymes with *fa*, a character often used in words meaning 'prosperous'), the opening ceremonies kick off at 8pm on 8 August 2008. Moviemakers Steven Spielberg, Ang Lee and Zhang Yimou, as well as American music producer Quincy Jones, are among the artistic directors for the opening and closing ceremonies.

The event program was not finalised at the time of writing, but a preliminary schedule had football (soccer) finals slated for noon on 23 August (admission Y200 to Y800); the women's marathon final for 7.30am on 17 August (admission free) and the men's marathon final for 7.30am on 24 August (admission free). Check the **Olympics** (http://en.beijing2008.cn) website for details.

You can buy tickets from the official Olympics ticket distributor in your country of residence. Visit http://en.beijing2008.cn/tickets for a complete list or contact your local Olympic committee for information. Tickets will be on sale during the Games but many popular events may be sold out by then.

Tickets are required for most competitions. Admission to preliminary events averages Y50 to Y200; finals average Y200 to Y800. Spectators can line the roads and watch the following events for free: cycling road races (men's 11am 9 August, women's 2pm 10 August) and the marathon finals (men's 7.30am 24 August, women's 7.30am 17 August). Giant TV screens may also be put in public parks so people can watch stadium events for free, but nothing was confirmed at the time of writing.

>HISTORICAL HOTSPOTS

Great Wall at Simatai (p109)

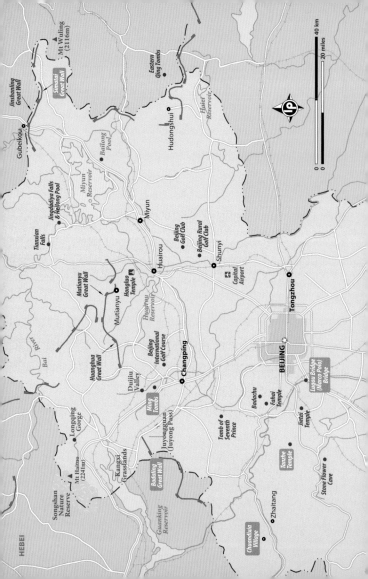

THE GREAT WALL 长城

No matter how often you've heard about it, or how many pictures you've seen, the Great Wall will still awe you when you finally lay eyes on it.

The long and complicated history of the structure adds to its mystique. The ancient Chinese had always fortified their cities and states with enormous walls. By 290 BC, China's northern frontier was pocked with defensive structures. When Mongolian nomads began sabre rattling on China's doorstep in 224 BC, Emperor Qin (221–207 BC) linked some of these structures into a mega-wall. By the time thousands of labourers finished work in 214 BC, China had the most awesome military barrier the world had seen.

However, by the time the Sui dynasty (AD 589–1279) arrived, the wall was a crumbling mess. It was rebuilt, but the lengthy wall was difficult to man and the Mongols swept into China. Years later, the Mings (1368–1644) overhauled the wall again, ditching the rammed earth used in the first versions in favour of bricks and stone slabs.

Looking back, the wall didn't repel foreign invaders as well as successive emperors had planned, but its function as a signal post was invaluable. On many occasions, watchtower sentries were able to warn the capital about enemy troop movements by burning wolf-dung to send smoke signals.

These days, sections of the wall are found as far west as China's Xinjiang province and as far east as the North Korean border. Much of it is in disrepair, and despite government conservation efforts, the wall is still plundered for building materials in some remote areas. Near Beijing, sections of the wall have been developed for tourism and renovated to varying degrees.

Depending on the type of experience you want, the Badaling (p108) or Simatai (p109) sections of the wall, both built during the Ming dynasty, are excellent choices for a visit.

COMMUNE AT THE GREAT WALL

For something a little different, check out the **Commune at the Great Wall** (☎ 5878 8328; www.commune.com.cn; Badaling; tours Y120), 70km northwest of Beijing. It's one of the most offbeat hotels in Beijing and an outstanding example of contemporary architecture. High-rollers can stay in one of the 46 guest rooms spread among 11 luxury 'villas'. For everyone else, the Commune can be experienced on a guided tour, which will take you through the grounds and any unoccupied rooms. You must reserve a place on the tour in advance.

BADALING GREAT WALL
八达岭长城

It may get slagged for its commercialisation, but Badaling still has plenty of reasons to recommend it. The hilly scenery is lovely, and as the closest section of the wall to Beijing, Badaling is ideal for those with limited time. Leave early and it can be done as a half-day trip.

Heavily renovated (and overrun with hawkers, souvenir vendors and snack stands), some people find the wall here isn't as 'wild' as they'd like. However, these repairs have made Badaling one of the most manageable sections of the wall for older travellers, families with small children, and those unable (or unwilling) to take on the crumbling stones and sheer drops of other wall sections.

The walk from the parking lot to the wall is fairly easy going. Cable cars are also available to take you up. Closer to ground, you can visit the **Great Wall Circle Vision Theatre** and the **Great Wall Museum**. At the time of research both were closed for Olympic makeovers but they should be reopened by the time you make it out here.

If visiting in summer, try to get to Badaling during the week; on weekends, the crush of visitors can be suffocating.

INFORMATION
Location 70km northwest of Beijing
Getting there 🚌 Tour Bus (p146)
Contact ☎ 6912 1338/2222
Costs admission Y45; an audio guide is Y40 with a Y100 deposit
When to go 🕙 7am-6pm

SIMATAI GREAT WALL
司马台长城

If you're fit, have sturdy shoes with good grip and want to experience the wall at one of its steepest and most beautiful points, Simatai is for you.

Simatai Great Wall has been partially renovated but several sections remain rough and rocky and have dramatic dips and rises. You'll need your arms free while climbing up and down so bring a day pack for your belongings. Drinks are sold on the wall but are very expensive. Food is less common so bring some snacks.

Take the **cable car** (1-way/round-trip Y30/50; 8.30am-4.30pm) up, which takes 15 minutes, followed by the so-called **mini-train** (1-way/round-trip Y30/20), a five-minute ride in what is actually an open funicular.

After that, the wall is a 10-minute walk up. From there, the wall undulates downhill towards the parking lot. Most people take two to three hours to walk this section. At the end, either walk downhill (20 to 30 minutes) or take the zip-line (Y35, three minutes) over the river to get to the exit. Alternatively cross the bridge (Y5) and remount the wall for more exploring.

Legendary for tenacity, Simatai souvenir vendors routinely follow hikers the length of the wall to make a sale. Unless you really *do* want that Great Wall calendar, the less eye contact the better.

INFORMATION
Location 110km northeast of Beijing
Getting there Tour Bus (p146)
Contact 6903 1051/5022; www.simatai-greatwall.net
Costs admission Y40; an audio guide is Y10 with a Y100 deposit
When to go 8am-5pm

MING TOMBS 明十三陵

Ming emperors believed in going out with a bang. So from 1409 until the fall of the dynasty in 1644, they had themselves buried here with their wives, concubines, imperial treasures and plenty of pomp and ceremony.

In all, 13 of the 16 Ming emperors are entombed here. (The other rulers missed out on the fun for various reasons: one wasn't yet ruling from Beijing, another disappeared during battle and yet another didn't consider himself worthy.)

Today, three of the tomb grounds are open to the public. **Ding Ling** is the tomb area of Emperor Wan Li (1563–1620). Visitors usually enjoy this crypt most, as it's the only one you can go inside. The other tomb grounds open to the public are **Chang Ling**, the resting place of Emperor Yongle, and **Zhao Ling**, where Emperor Longqing is buried.

The so-called **Spirit Way** (1 Apr-31 Oct Y30, 1 Nov-31 Mar Y20) is a 7km foot-road that leads to the crypt grounds. Lined with imposing stone statues of animals and court officials, it's considered the highlight of the Ming Tombs by many. Every other animal is in the crouching position and is said to rise at midnight during the 'changing of the guard'.

Other than the Spirit Way, the Ming Tombs aren't visually impressive at first. It's really the historical stories that make them come alive. A good guide makes all the difference so consider joining an English-language tour (p154). Be aware that group tours never take in all the tombs and usually stop at only one or two of the four sights mentioned above (usually Ding Ling and the Spirit Way).

INFORMATION

Location 50km north of Beijing
Getting there 🚌 Tour Bus (p146)
Contact ☎ 6076 1424
Costs Ding Ling Y60, Chang Ling Y45, Zhao Ling Y30
When to go ⏱ 8.30am-6.30pm, last entry 5.30pm

LUGOU BRIDGE (MARCO POLO BRIDGE) 卢沟桥

Built in 1189, Beijing's oldest marble bridge spans 266m across the Yongding River and sports hundreds of small but uniquely carved stone lions. They say no two lions are the same and their images grace hundreds of postcards and calendars.

When in China, Marco Polo was impressed enough with the bridge to mention it in his journals, so it became known as 'Marco Polo Bridge'.

However, in Asia the bridge is famous as the site of a 1937 battle that took place after Japanese troops illegally occupied a nearby railway junction. Chinese soldiers retaliated with gunfire, giving Japan its pretext for attacking Beijing and igniting full-scale war.

City officials have big plans for this sight, which include opening a museum and an 'old-style' shopping street here in time for the Olympics.

INFORMATION
Location Mentougou District, 门头沟区, 45km west of Beijing
Getting there Ⓜ Pingguoyuan, then bus 931 (Y6, 60 minutes, every 30 to 40 minutes 6.50am to 5.35pm); note that the last bus from Tanzhe Temple to the subway leaves at 5pm; you could also negotiate a taxi (bargaining starts around Y30 to Y40 one-way)
Contact ☎ 6086 2500
Costs admission Y35, or Y40 including Guanyin Caves
When to go ⌚ 8am-5.30pm 1 May-31 Oct, 8am-4.30pm 1 Nov-31 Apr

HISTORICAL HOTSPOTS

TANZHE TEMPLE 潭柘寺

Sprawling up a hill, and draped in shade, Beijing's oldest and largest temple retains a sense of gravitas despite being developed for tourism. Dating back to the Jin dynasty (AD 265–420), locals have traditionally come to this temple to pray for rain during droughts, or to harvest Cudrania trees, which provide yellow dye and nourish silkworms.

Once inside there are well over a dozen different pavilions and halls to visit. Check out the gory fate of hell-bound mortals at the **Dizang Hall**, visit the smoky **Guanyin Cave**, where you can taste spring-water tea or, for Y5, stroke the hanging **Stone Fish** for luck.

INFORMATION
Location 17km southwest of Beijing
Getting there 🚌 301 from Qianmen (Y2, 45 to 60 minutes) or taxi
Contact ☎ 8389 4614
Costs adult/child Y20/10
When to go 🕗 8am-5pm

CHUANDIXIA VILLAGE
川底下村

First settled in the early 1400s, this Ming-dynasty village is a favourite of travellers (and movie directors) for its 70-odd traditional courtyard homes, terraced orchards and beautiful stone alleyways.

Chuandixia has retained its old-world character thanks to its isolated location. Once an important stop on a trading route, village elders say the boom days ended when a highway was built near Zhaitang. Young people have picked up jobs elsewhere ever since, the elders say. For visitors, however, the village and its hilly surroundings are still lovely places to explore.

Courtyard homes here are still tattooed with Maoist graffiti (usually in the form of big red Chinese characters) left over from the Cultural Revolution. Slogans such as 'Arm our Minds with Mao Zedong Thought' and 'Proletariats of the World Unite!', though faded, remain on many walls.

Several Chinese miniseries and TV shows are shot here each year. The dozens of small caves pocking the hillside were all built for a recent movie shoot.

So far, the village council has done a good job handling tourism development in Chuandixia. Though there's now plenty of places to eat and even a small souvenir shop, it's all been done discreetly, maintaining the place's charm.

INFORMATION

Location 91km west of Beijing
Getting there ☺ Pingguoyuan, then bus 929 (branch line 支线) to Zhaitang (斋堂, Y7, two to three hours), then taxi van (Y15, 15 to 20 minutes); the last bus from Zhaitang to Pingguoyuan leaves at 4.20pm. If taking public transport out here seems too daunting, keep an eye out for tours. The China Culture Club, p154, runs an excellent one (Y200), usually once a month.
Contact ☎ 6981 9333; www.cuandixia.com
Costs admission Y20
When to go ☾ ticket office 9am-6pm

>SNAPSHOTS

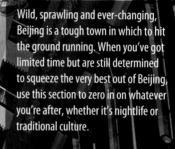

Wild, sprawling and ever-changing, Beijing is a tough town in which to hit the ground running. When you've got limited time but are still determined to squeeze the very best out of Beijing, use this section to zero in on whatever you're after, whether it's nightlife or traditional culture.

Not for acrophobes – a shopping plaza on Wangfujing Dajie (p38)

ACCOMMODATION

As Beijing gets ready for you-know-when, hotels are being thrown up faster than ever. Rooms in all price brackets are readily available.

Luxury options are all over the city. Almost all major hotel chains (that aren't already here) are opening new properties in advance of the Olympics, including **Sofitel** (www.sofitel.com) and the **Ritz-Carlton** (www.ritzcarlton.com). In foreign-owned hotels, service and amenities are what you'd expect, with modern business centres, English-speaking staff and tour services. However, Chinese-owned luxury hotels won't necessarily have English-speaking staff and facilities can be a little less polished.

Beijing's midrange hotels haven't got much attention in the run-up to 2008. They're everywhere and are generally unremarkable. Facilities are often old, amenities are limited and staff frequently don't speak English.

A happy exception to this rule are courtyard hotels, which usually boast atmosphere, history and a good level of service. Often located in Beijing's traditional *hutong* (alleyway) neighbourhoods, rooms in these popular hotels are usually booked weeks in advance. Reservations are a must, especially in summer. Motel-style chains, though generic, are also good midrange choices. They may not have much Chinese flavour, but the service is good and the facilities clean and modern. Two ubiquitous chains in Beijing are **Home Inn** (www.homeinns.com) and **Comfort Inn** (www.comfortinn.com).

Beijing's budget hotels are generally pretty shabby and have no English-speaking staff. Hostels, however, are mushrooming all over central Beijing (particularly in Dongcheng, Map pp40–1, and Xicheng's Houhai Lake area, Map p87, D2) and are a terrific option. Staff usually

Need a place to stay? Find and book it at lonelyplanet.com. Over 40 properties are featured for Beijing – each personally visited, thoroughly reviewed and happily recommended by a Lonely Planet author. From hostels to high-end hotels, we've hunted out the places that will bring you unique and special experiences. Read independent reviews by authors and other travellers, and get practical information including amenities, maps and photos. Then reserve your room simply and securely via Hotels & Hostels – our online booking service. It's all at lonelyplanet.com/hotels.

speak good English and visitor information and tour services are among the best in the city.

While in Beijing, travellers often base themselves in Dongcheng, Xicheng or North Chaoyang. Dongcheng (p38) has many of Beijing's major sights including Tiananmen Square, the Forbidden City and the Wangfujing shopping street. Many of the city's popular luxury hotels sit in this district.

West of Dongcheng, Xicheng (p86) has a good number of hostels and midrange accommodation and gets you near the Houhai Lake area's bars, restaurants and shopping. East of Dongcheng, North Chaoyang (p52) has the city's biggest nightlife areas, best restaurants and most popular markets. Hostels and midrange and luxury options are everywhere.

Never assume the hotel's listed rates are its actual prices. Hotels usually slash these by 40% to 50% in all but the busiest times of the year and during holidays like the Spring Festival/Chinese New Year (p26). You are expected to bargain so don't be shy about asking for a discount.

Peak season for Chinese tourists is July and August, when midrange and budget hotels are busy. Peak season for foreign travellers is September and October, when top-end hotels fill and charge closer to their posted rates. In winter you can often strike great hotel bargains. If staying in Beijing over Spring Festival, book ahead, rooms can be reserved months in advance.

When checking-in, guests fill out a registration form with their visa and passport details. The form is then sent to the local Public Security Bureau.

BEST FOR LUXURY

> Grand Hyatt (www.beijing.grand
  .hyatt.com)
> St-Regis (www.stregis.com/beijing)
> Peninsula Beijing (http://beijing
  .peninsula.com)
> Kerry Centre (www.shangri-la.com
  /en/property/beijing/kerrycentre)

BEST COURTYARD HOTELS

> Bamboo Garden (www.bbgh.com.cn)
> Lusongyuan Hotel (www.the-silk
  -road.com/hotel/lusongyuanhotel)
> Haoyuan Hotel (www.haoyuanhotel
  .com)

BEST HOSTELS

> Far East Youth Hostel (www.fareastyh
  .com)
> Peking Downtown Backpackers
  Association (www.backpackingchina
  .com)
> Drum & Bell (☎ 8610 6403
  7702/9907)

MOST UNFORGETTABLE ATMOSPHERE

> Commune at the Great Wall (www
  .commune.com.cn)
> Red Capital Residence (www.red
  capitalclub.com.cn)

ARCHITECTURE

Beijing leapfrogged from the one-of-a-kind traditional architecture of the Ming and Qing dynasties to the horrors of socialist-realist design in the 1950s. Lately it's been throwing up buildings that are so daring, they couldn't be built in most other countries.

Besides obvious sights like the Forbidden City (p44) or the Temple of Heaven (p18), the best of Beijing's traditional architecture is its courtyard homes found in the city's *hutong* (alleyways). These homes are built on a north–south axis with living quarters wrapped around a small courtyard. All are built in strict accordance with feng shui principles to ensure the *qi* (energy) can freely circulate. There are no outside windows, so when the courtyard gates are shut, it becomes an individual private world.

Every Ming and Qing building, no matter how big or small, is built along the same principles, though wealthier people add more pavilions and space. Architecturally speaking, some describe the Forbidden City as the biggest courtyard house of them all.

There are no known buildings that predate the Ming dynasty in Beijing (except some portions of the Great Wall). And though there are plenty of Ming structures around town, most have been rebuilt as fire and weather have taken their toll over the centuries.

From the 1950s on, socialist-realist architecture was in vogue. Soviet architects descended on Beijing to help their 'socialist brothers' modernise the capital. They hoped to create a skyline pocked with Stalin's so-called 'Wedding Cake' buildings. Much architecture from this period is now being torn down, though some examples remain.

The Beijing Exhibition Hall is still an active business hub in Xicheng. In Dongcheng, the hulking China National Museum (closed for renovations until 2009) opened in 1959, built to commemorate the 10th anniversary of the founding of the People's Republic of China. The Great Hall of the People, also built in 1959, is perhaps the most imposing structure left over from this period, and it almost wasn't finished. The Soviet builders packed up and went home after the Sino-Soviet split, leaving before they put the roof on. For more details on modern architecture, see p17.

BEST SOCIALIST ARCHITECTURE
> Beijing Exhibition Hall (p88)
> Great Hall of the People (p42)
> China National Museum (Map pp40–1, B8)

BEST TRADITIONAL ARCHITECTURE
> Huguang Guildhall (p99)
> Prince Gong's Residence (p89)
> Mei Lanfang Former Residence (p89)

> Drum and Bell Towers (p42 and p39)
> Chuandixia Village (p113)

MOST CONTROVERSIAL NEW BUILDINGS
> National Grand Theatre (p92)
> CCTV Building (p74)

MOST EMBRACED NEW BUILDINGS
> Capital Museum (p88)
> Bird's Nest Stadium (p17)

Above Some things are better in threes: the Xizhimen subway buildings

DRINKING

Beijing's always been good for low-key bars and no-frills pubs. More recently, however, a number of chic new bars and lounges are paying as much attention to the décor as they are to the drinks, giving the city's nightlife some much-needed pizzazz.

Once Beijing's famous nightlife hub, Sanlitun Lu (between Gongrentiyuchang Beilu and Dongzhimenwai Dajie, Map pp54–5, D4) has faded off the radar. Though still lined with dozens of bars, most are considered touristy and not worth visiting. It's the lanes off Sanlitun Lu that have the most exciting new nightlife additions with smart, sophisticated lounges catering to older business crowds just around the corner from rowdy bars geared to teenagers.

Elsewhere, the Houhai Lake area (Map p87, D2) has countless bars, many with lovely lakeside views. You need to be discerning here: lots of new places have opened to cash in on Houhai's popularity but they aren't necessarily strong in the drink quality or service departments. However, it's pretty easy to tell which ones these places are by the touts who try to block the way and physically pull patrons into the bar. Dongcheng is another great area for low-key, stylish bars, particularly around the Drum and Bell Towers and along Nanluogu Xiang (Map pp40–1, B3).

Another exciting hang-out area is around the Wudaokou light-rail stop and along Chengfu Lu (Map p81, B2) where the large student population keeps dozens of great bars afloat. Most of these have a mix of Chinese and foreign students inside.

Most average Chinese would rather go sing karaoke on a Friday night or share a Y2 beer and some street food than drop Y40 on a fancy lounge cocktail. But this is changing, meaning you'll increasingly find a good mix of locals and expats in bars. Elsewhere, a young, more worldly generation of Chinese, many of them artists and musicians, are opening modest places with plenty of atmosphere and are slowly overtaking the stale karaoke-pumping, *baijiu*-slinging drinking holes of the past.

The free English-language listings and entertainment magazines are the best way to find out about what's new in town, particularly *That's Beijing* (www.thatsbj.com/blog), *Time Out Beijing*, *Beijing This Month* and *City Weekend*.

BEST TO IMPRESS
> Centro (p77)
> Lan (p79)
> Q Bar (p63)
> Bed Bar (p50)

BEST FOR RELAXING
> Stone Boat Bar (p79)
> No Name Bar (p92)
> Drum & Bell (p50)
> Beer Mania (p61)

Top left Rickshaw (p63), a prime spot for post-sightseeing debriefs **Above** No Name Bar (p92), a contradiction in terms

FOOD

Food is arguably Beijingers favourite social activity and it's not uncommon for locals to greet you with an enthusiastic *chifan le ma?* (have you eaten food yet?) instead of 'how are you?'

There are thousands of food stalls and restaurants (many with an international reputation) all over the city. International cuisine is well-represented, as is the cuisine of every province and region of the country. It's the ideal situation for foodies: you can literally eat your way across China and never leave Beijing. Chinese cuisine has four main 'schools', one for each compass point.

Beijing or 'northern cuisine' is heavy on the wheat and millet, making noodles, steamed dumplings *(jiaozi)* and steamed buns popular staples. Peking duck (p21) is the city's most famous dish. For locals, however, nothing beats Beijing's street food or 'Beijing snacks' *(Beijing xiaochi*, 北京小吃), which involve anything that can be whipped up roadside or skewered on a stick. Going out with friends and scooping up these cheap eats is as much a social activity as a way to quell hunger.

Some of China's other star cuisines include Sichuan (western cuisine), Cantonese (southern cuisine) and Shanghai (eastern cuisine). Shanghai cuisine abounds in fish, fresh vegetables and light flavours. Sichuan dishes are heavy on pork, chicken, tofu, bamboo and mushrooms, and are known for their tongue-searing red chilli and flower pepper ingredients. Cantonese food is much more exotic – there's a saying that the only four-legged thing not eaten is the table – and food preparation is far more complex. Dishes are often sweeter than other cuisines and much less spicy.

Dining Chinese-style is a noisy and often messy affair with people gathered around big, round tables. Beijingers don't use décor or service to determine whether a restaurant is good or bad – for them it's only the food and company that counts. Going out with a big group is considered ideal, as is loading up the table with more dishes than can possibly be eaten. Don't be surprised if your Chinese host occasionally puts a small amount of food on your plate with their chopsticks before serving themselves; this is considered polite.

BEST PEKING DUCK
> Beijing Dadong Roast Duck Restaurant (p59)
> Quanjude Roast Duck Restaurant (p48)
> Made in China (p48)
> Liqun Roast Duck Restaurant (p71)
> Bianyifang Roast Duck Restaurant (p70)

BEST FOR ROMANCE
> Courtyard (p48)
> Source (p49)
> Nuage (p91)

MOST MEMORABLE ATMOSPHERE
> Green T House (p60)
> Red Capital Club (p49)
> Fangshan Restaurant (p91)
> Baguo Buyi (p48)
> Haitanghua Pyongyang Cold Noodle Restaurant (p60)

BEST STREET FOOD
> Donghuamen Night Market (p48)
> Wangfujing Snack Street (p49)
> Ghost Street (p49)

Top left Buddhism and vegetarianism meet at Xu Xiang Zhai Vegetarian Restaurant (p50)

PARKS & GARDENS

Many of Beijing's parks are former imperial gardens, off-limits to regular Beijingers for centuries and opened to the public only after the founding of the People's Republic of China. In Dongcheng district, Beihai and Jingshan Parks were both once part of the Forbidden City. The hill in Jingshan Park (p42), which is not a natural feature, was built to protect the palace from the evil spirits coming from the north. Jingshan Park is also the place where Emperor Chongzhen hung himself from a locust tree as rebels swarmed at the city walls. Nearby, Beihai Park has been a royal stomping ground since the Yuan dynasty, when earth was removed to make the enormous lake you see here today. The displaced soil was used to make the small middle island, Jade Islet.

Elsewhere, the majority of the city's parks were created from land formerly used by the emperors to perform annual rites to various gods. Though each of the parks are different, all still have the vast altars where the emperors stood while conducting their rituals. These days, however, locals use the altars for kite flying and taichi practice.

But Chinese parks and gardens are more than just recreational spaces; they are considered to be landscape art, meant to perfectly balance the yin and yang. Each garden must have several elements – the main ones being plants, rock, water and pavilions – in order to make it harmonious. The gardens are built as much for promoting the flow of *qi* as they are to be an aesthetic pleasure. The hardness of the rock (yang) should balance out the softness of the water (yin). Plants are chosen for their symbolic significance as much as for their aesthetics.

BEST ESCAPES FROM POLLUTION
> Fragrant Hills Park (p82)
> Beijing Botanic Gardens (p82)

BEST FORMER RITUAL GROUNDS
> Temple of Heaven Park (p69)
> Workers' Cultural Palace (p43)
> Ritan Park (p74)
> Ditan Park (p42)

MOST BEAUTIFUL LANDSCAPES
> Grand View Garden (above; p96)
> Old Summer Palace Park (p82)

BEST ROMANTIC WALKS
> Summer Palace (p83)
> Beihai Park (p88)
> Zhongshan Park (p46)
> Longtan Park (p68)

SHOPPING

Shopping is one of Beijing's pleasures – whether you're looking for souvenirs, haggling over pearls or just soaking up the atmosphere at one of the open-air markets. Prices aren't as cheap as they used to be, but good deals are still possible for items like art, scrolls, silk, jewellery, jade and clothing.

Beijing has a staggering amount of stores and shopping districts to choose from. Xuanwu's two pedestrian streets are among the most popular. Liulichang Xijie and Liulichang Dongjie (Map p95, C2), located in a vibrant *hutong* neighbourhood, are done up as old-style shopping streets with dozens of stores specialising in inks, paintings and chop making. This is where Beijing's professional calligraphers, teachers and students come to buy their paper, brushes and calligraphy books. Nearby, Dazhalan Jie (Map p95, D2) hangs on to its traditional character and is home to some of Beijing's oldest businesses.

In Dongcheng, the pedestrianised Wangfujing Dajie is the most fashionable shopping strip, anchored by the luxury Oriental Plaza mall and bordered by towering department stores.

Next door in Chaoyang, clothing from the Silk Market or Yaxiu Clothing Market is still many travellers' favourite buy, though be on the look-out for shoddy workmanship.

In Xicheng, you'll find lots of clothing and jewellery stalls and stores in the Houhai Lake area (Map p87, D2), particularly around Qianhai Lake and Yandai Xiejie. During summer, vendors also set up along the lakeside, hawking illuminated, coloured lanterns, a particularly popular souvenir.

Elsewhere, Xidan Beidajie (北大街, Map p87, C5), just north of the Xidan subway stop, is a chaotic shopping strip packed with above- and below-ground malls and department stores. Locals mob it on weekends.

While handicrafts and kites, traditional paper cuttings and silk scarves all make excellent souvenirs, beware of buying anything the vendor claims is 'antique'. It's illegal for foreigners to take anything made before 1795 out of the country, and the fact is that there are very few antiques left on the market. What wasn't destroyed or stolen in the late-19th and early-20th-century wars was usually taken care of during the Cultural Revolution. However, this doesn't stop vendors from swearing they've got a Song dynasty vase with your name on it.

The same goes for art: almost 100% of all works from China's great

20th-century masters are completely catalogued in private collections and museums. That guy at the Panjiayuan Antique Market claiming he has an original 'Qi Baishi' should be treated with scepticism.

Prices are fixed in malls and department stores, though, if you ask, a 10% discount is sometimes given. Markets and antique shops, where bargaining is a time-honoured tradition, are another matter. The old rule about halving the vendor's asking price to make your counteroffer no longer holds true. Foreigners have been throwing money around Beijing for years, and many vendors start as high as 10 times the going rate when bargaining with travellers, especially at places like the Silk Market and Panjiayuan. No matter how much they try to overcharge you, remember to keep it friendly. The point of bargaining is not to fight but to find a price acceptable to both parties. Walking away sometimes gets vendors to lower their price.

To keep up with customer spending sprees, closing time is fading further into the night. Most malls and chain shops are open seven days, from 9am or 10am until 10pm, as are many of the boutiques around Sanlitun Lu.

In many department stores and older shops, the communist system of changing money for goods continues. You decide what you want, then you're given a ticket to give to a cashier who collects your money and gives you a stamped receipt to return to the salesperson in exchange for your purchase.

Many large department stores and upscale malls take international credit cards like Visa; medium- and smaller-sized stores only take Chinese credit cards, if they accept them at all. Markets are cash-only, so come prepared.

BEST WINDOW-SHOPPING
> Dazhalan Jie (Map p95, D2)
> Liulichang Xijie and Liulichang Dongjie (Map p95, C2)
> Wangfujing Dajie (Map pp40–1, C6)

MOST FUN FOR HAGGLING
> Pearl Market (p70)
> Silk Market (p76)
> Yaxiu Clothing Market (p57)
> Jayi Clothing Market (p57)
> Beijing Curio City (p74)

BEST MARKET ATMOSPHERE
> Panjiayuan Antique Market (p75)
> Dongjiao Shichang (p74)

BEST SOUVENIRS
> Plastered T-Shirts (p47)
> Mu Handcrafts (p89)
> Ten Fu's Tea (p47)
> Sanshizhai Kites (p47)
> Timezone 8 Art Books (p56)

ACROBATICS

Chinese acrobatic shows are always a thrill and Beijing's troupes are excellent. There's nothing quite like seeing young contortionists turn themselves inside out and upside down while spinning plates on the ends of long sticks.

Circus acts have a 2000-year history in China. Even scholars as far back as the Warring States Period (roughly 475–221 BC) took pains to mention off-beat activities like dagger juggling and stilt-walking.

Routines were developed using simple everyday objects like sticks, hoops, chairs and jars. Difficult acts to follow include 'Peacock Displaying its Feathers' (a dozen or more people balanced on one bicycle) and 'Pagoda of Bowls' (a performer does everything with her torso except tie it in knots, while balancing a stack of bowls on her foot, head, or both).

Despite these superhuman feats, acrobats weren't always respected by Chinese nobility and the upper classes. That all changed in the 20th century, however, especially once Chinese troupes (particularly from Beijing) started performing abroad to international acclaim.

Now, professional Chinese acrobats undergo the same rigorous training as future sports superstars. Programs start before age 10, when gifted children are singled out, scooped up and enrolled by their parents in schools run by the various acrobatic companies. The typical acrobat retires from their performing career sometime in their 30s.

Popular acrobatic venues in Beijing include the Liyuan Theatre (p100) and the Chaoyang Theatre (p64). Some travellers prefer the Tianqiao Acrobatics Theatre (p100) for its small stage and a chance to see the performers close-up.

CYCLING

Experiencing Beijing by bike is not to be missed. The city is as flat as a pancake, bike lanes are everywhere and if you can put up with the exhaust fumes and insane drivers, it's one of the most enjoyable ways to get around the city.

Some of the nicest areas to ride are the *hutong*, especially around the Houhai Lake area (Map p87, D2), and the neighbourhood around the Drum and Bell Towers and Nanluogu Xiang (Map pp40–1, B3).

Rentals are everywhere, but your safest bet is at your accommodation. If not, bike rentals are common around Houhai Lake, as well as any *hutong* near a youth hostel or courtyard hotel. They usually charge Y20 to Y30 per day. Always check the bike out well before you leave and never leave your passport for the deposit instead of a cash deposit.

Theft is a serious problem in Beijing so always park your bike in the city's cycling parks (5 mao). They are staffed by an attendant who keeps track of the bike comings and goings.

Be extremely careful when driving at night and remember the Beijing rule: it's always the cyclist's job to get out of the car's way and not the other way around.

GALLERIES

As little as five years ago, Beijing had the Red Gate Gallery and little else. These days the scene has exploded, most notably with the success of the Factory 798/Dashanzi Art District (p56) located in the far northeast of Chaoyang district.

When it opened, Factory 798 housed just five galleries. Today, it is home to over 100 and counting, with a slew of heavy-hitting international galleries setting up shop alongside local avant-garde specialists. Though some decry its popularity, nobody argues against Factory 798 still being *the* place to head to for what's new and exciting in contemporary art, particularly if you have a hankering for experimental art, media installations or large-scale sculpture.

Despite the unquenchable art market and a new generation of seemingly insatiable Chinese collectors, few new galleries are opening in central Beijing. Instead, artists' collectives and gallery owners looking for the next big thing are moving even *further* away into Beijing's far-flung suburbs.

However, if you want to stick closer to town, there are a handful of established galleries in central Beijing (within the Second Ring Rd) that continue to thrive. Galleries here tend to feature selections of representational contemporary art alongside abstract art and sculpture.

BEST FOR SCOPING OUT UP-AND-COMERS
> C5Art (p53)
> Creation Gallery (p74)

MOST CHALLENGING NEW EXHIBITS
> Beijing Commune (p56)

BEST FOR CHECKING OUT ESTABLISHED ARTISTS
> Red Gate Gallery (p68)
> White Space Gallery (p56)
> Wan Fung Art Gallery (p43)

GAY & LESBIAN

It had all seemed so promising just a few years ago with new gay clubs opening steadily and many existing clubs adding gay- and lesbian-friendly nights to their calendars. Unfortunately, many of these clubs have disappeared in the last two years, victims of the modernisation wrecking-ball that has sent so many bars and restaurants scattering as roads are widened and shiny new buildings go up. The gay and lesbian scene was so tiny to begin with that it still hasn't recovered, though the stalwarts of the scene survive. Destination (p65), Beijing's only gay club, is still going strong, as is West Wing (p92), which caters to lesbians. Pipe's Café (p63) is also continuing with its lesbian-friendly Saturday nights.

Apart from these spots, the gay and lesbian scene in Beijing is low-key. Despite small progress (there was an International Gay and Lesbian Film Festival in Beijing in 2005), Chinese authorities still take a dim view of homosexuality. The Chinese Psychiatric Association only declassified homosexuality as a mental disorder in 2001 and many still consider it a 'Western problem'.

For newcomers to the city, finding gay or gay-friendly nightclubs can be a challenge. Check out the *Utopia Guide to China* by John Goss or check www.utopia-asia.com/chinbeij.htm for tips on where to go.

MARTIAL ARTS

Martial arts are as much a part of the Beijing landscape as *hutong*, temples and bicycles. Hit any city park by sunrise and you'll see droves of Beijingers jabbing, kicking and slicing through the air.

There are three main martial arts and exercises popular in China: *taiji-quan* (taichi), which is known for its slow, fluid movements; *gongfu* (kung-fu), which is famous for its focus on self-defence; and *qigong*, which is associated with traditional Chinese medicine, focusing on mental and physical wellbeing.

Taichi is the most popular. The yang style, with its uniform pacing, is the style most Beijingers practise. But walk around town and you'll also see lots of wu-style practitioners with their smaller and more pronounced stances and motions. Chen-style taichi is the easiest to recognise and the most fun to watch as practitioners perform slow-as-molasses forms before exploding into quick, powerful movements.

To try some yourself, the **Jinghua Wushu Association** (京华武术协会; Map pp54-5, E2; ☎ 6465 3388; Kempinski Hotel, Liangmaqiao Lu, 亮马桥凯宾斯基饭店; Ⓜ Donzhimen, then taxi) gives English-language lessons (Y90 per session). The China Culture Club (p154) also offers occasional one-off classes that include anything from beginners taichi to *taijijian* (taichi with swords) at the Altar of the Earth at Ditan Park (p42).

To simply watch, get to the Temple of Heaven Park (p69) at 6am, where crowds of taichi practitioners gather to sway and lunge as the sun rises. With a turnout regularly in the hundreds, it's a sight worth waking up for. If you're not a morning person, you can check out some death-defying martial arts moves at the Red Theatre's (p71) spectacular show: *The Legend of Kung-Fu*.

MUSEUMS

Beijing's museum scene is picking up. While the city has countless cultural institutions covering everything from architecture to stone carvings, most still aren't very foreigner-friendly, with unilingual staff and Chinese-only labelling or obscure Ching-lish captions. However, several museums have got their act together in recent years, putting together thoughtful exhibits with English captions, as well as getting spiffy new English audio guides. The new Capital Museum is the most spectacular of them all and rivals anything you might see in London or New York.

Most of Beijing's interesting museums are in central Beijing or near Dongcheng district. Heavy-hitters such as the China National Museum (closed for repairs until 2009) are here, as well as many smaller museums hidden in historical buildings such as Qianmen or the Southeast Watchtower (p68). Remember that the **Forbidden City** (www.dpm.org.cn) is more than just an ancient palace and has dozens of ongoing exhibitions all over its grounds; check the website for a list of temporary exhibitions.

Xicheng's Houhai Lake area (Map p87, D2) also has some interesting museums. Here, there are dozens of small courtyard homes, formerly owned by notable Beijing writers and artists, which have been turned into small museums. Many lack enough English captions or context to be meaningful to foreigners, but the Mei Lanfang Former Residence is a notable exception.

MOST BEAUTIFUL EXHIBITIONS
> Capital Museum (p88)
> Poly Art Museum (p53)

BEST BEIJING HISTORY
> Beijing Imperial City Art Museum (p39)
> Qianmen (p43)
> Forbidden City's Imperial Treasure Gallery (p44)
> Summer Palace's Wenchang Gallery (p83)

BEST CONTEMPORARY ART
> National Art Museum of China (p43)

QUIRKIEST COLLECTIONS
> Mei Lanfang Former Residence (p89)
> Great Bell Temple (p82)
> Forbidden City's Clocks & Watches Gallery (p44)
> Temple of Heaven's Divine Music Administration (p69)

SNAPSHOTS

TEMPLES

Temples are found in every nook and cranny of Beijing, but don't fear getting 'templed out'. Beijing's best are all unique in their own way and it's worth taking the time to visit several. They are wonderfully atmospheric places with solemn worshippers, busy monks and plumes of smoking incense wafting through the air. Every school of Chinese thought is represented in Beijing, and Confucian, Taoist and Buddhist temples are ubiquitous throughout the city.

Whatever the school, Chinese temples are laid out in the same way as traditional courtyard homes (see also p118): along a north–south axis according to the principles of feng shui. The middle courtyard area contains the prayer halls while the surrounding quarters are usually the quarters of the resident monks.

Chongwen's colossal Temple of Heaven (p18) is the best known, along with Dongcheng's Lama Temple, which follows the Yellow Hat sect of Tibetan Buddhism. Around the corner from here is the Confucius Temple (p39), the country's second largest temple honouring the famous philosopher.

The differences between Beijing's Buddhist and Taoist temples aren't always immediately apparent, but the monks have distinctive appearances. Buddhist monks usually have shaved heads while Taoists have their long hair tied into a topknot.

Beijing's temples don't have strict rules for visitors but do not photograph monks or worshippers if you haven't asked for their permission.

MOST FRIGHTENING
> Dongyue Temple (p53)

BEST BUDDHIST
> Wuta Temple (p84)
> Sleeping Buddha Temple at the Beijing Botanic Gardens (p82)
> Fayuan Temple (p96)

BEST TAOIST
> White Cloud Temple (p89)

BEST TIBETAN
> Lama Temple (p42)
> Summer Palace's Four Great Regions (p83)

>BACKGROUND

Sculpted column in front of Tiananmen Gate (p43)

BACKGROUND

HISTORY

Located on a plain, prone to dust storms and containing no natural bodies of water, Beijing has got to be one of the oddest places in the world to establish a national capital. None of that seemed to bother Emperor Yongle (1360–1424), however, and despite the strikes against it, Yongle moved to this backwater location without hesitation and declared Beijing the capital of the Ming dynasty.

Much of what you see in today's Beijing is thanks to him, including the layout and iconic sights such as the Forbidden City and the Temple of Heaven.

The Mings also got busy outside town, overhauling the Great Wall to try to keep out the Manchus. Despite these efforts, the Manchus waltzed into town anyway, overthrew the Mings and established the Qing dynasty (1644–1911). The Qings added their own fingerprints to the city in the way of summer palaces, pagodas and temples. Though the Qing Dynasty disintegrated in its final years, many consider it to be one of Chinese history's great dynasties.

With invaders and rebels launching repeated attacks on the capital, the last years of the Qing were some of the most challenging Beijing had ever known. The city also bore the brunt of the Second Opium War (1856–60), the Taiping Rebellion (1851–64) and the Boxer Rebellion (1900).

THE COMMUNIST REVOLUTION

When Empress Cixi died in 1908, she bequeathed power to two-year-old Puyi (Aisin Gioro Puyi), who was China's last emperor. But the Qing dynasty, battered by years of war and power struggles, was effectively rudderless and quickly collapsed. The revolution of 1911 paved the way for the Kuomintang to take power and the Republic of China was declared, with Sun Yatsen as president. Warlords continued to carve up and rule the north of the country and foreigners controlled important economic zones in major ports like Shanghai and Tianjin.

Crippling poverty and splintered rule was a recipe for further rebellion. Beijing University bubbled with dissent and it was here that Karl Marx's *Communist Manifesto* found its way into the hands of a library assistant named Mao Zedong (1893–1976). The communists soon emerged and joined with the Kuomintang to wrestle power from the northern war-lords. The Kuomintang turned on the communists a year later (1927) and slaughtered them en masse. Communist survivors fled to the countryside and launched a civil war.

The Japanese invaded Beijing in 1937 and overran the east of China for the duration of WWII, causing the Kuomintang to flee west. After Japan's defeat by Allied forces in 1945, the Kuomintang returned to Beijing but its days were numbered; by this time the Chinese Civil War was in full swing, and in 1949 the communists, under the leadership of Mao, cheered 'Victory!' As the Kuomintang fled to Taiwan, the People's Liberation Army (PLA) marched into Beijing, where Mao proclaimed the People's Republic of China.

AFTERMATH

After 1949 came a period of catastrophic historical destruction in Beijing. The huge city walls were pulled down, hundreds of temples and monuments were destroyed and buildings were flattened. In 1966 Mao launched the Cultural Revolution and China was to remain in the grip of chaos for a decade.

Anything considered anti-proletarian was destroyed – from temples to the education system to countless people. Everyone was suspected of harbouring 'capitalist-roadster' thoughts, neighbours turned on one another and Mao's youth army, the Red Guard, terrorised the nation. The damage sustained during this era is still evident at many of Beijing's popular sights, though captions sometimes incorrectly attribute it to either 'foreign forces' or 'the Japanese'.

Mao died in 1976 and Deng Xiaoping, his former protégé, launched a modernisation drive. The country opened up and Westerners were given the chance to see what the communists had been up to for the past 30 years. The 1980s and '90s saw the restoration of temples, monuments and schools. Glittering towers and high-rises erupted. China decided to embrace modernity without altering politically. In 1989 pro-democracy student demonstrations took place in Tiananmen Square; the government's retaliation sent shivers through the world. Today there's a conspicuous absence of protest in Beijing. Political dissent exists, but unrelenting government coercion has consigned it to a deeply subterranean level.

In the run-up to the 2008 Olympic Games, the city has changed dramatically both physically and socially. City officials want to put Beijing's

BACKGROUND

FENG SHUI

Literally meaning 'wind and water', feng shui is a collection of ancient geomantic principles that see bodies of water and landforms directing the cosmic currents of the universal *qi* (energy). Feng shui guidelines create a positive path for *qi*, which can maximise a person's wealth, happiness, longevity and fertility. Ignoring the principles and blocking the flow can spell disaster. Temples, tombs, houses and even whole cities have been built in feng shui fashion to harmonise with the surrounding landscape. Within a building, the order of rooms and arrangement of furniture can also inhibit or enhance *qi* flow. The construction of high-rises and new roads throughout Beijing has incensed some residents, who believe the balance of the geography is being disturbed.

best foot forward for the world and are taking baby steps towards openness and transparency, though many believe that once the world has left, things will go back to the way they were before, leaving Beijing straddling two very different currents – communism and capitalism – as it takes its place on the world stage.

LIFE AS A BEIJINGER

With the modern rubbing up against the traditional, it's a dynamic time to be a Beijinger. Young people have more freedom than ever before and are experimenting with everything from fashion to music to putting off marriage and children until well into their 30s. Meanwhile, their parents struggle to adapt to changes they never believed they'd see in their lifetimes. In a city suddenly flush with cash, many are launching businesses in order to get ahead. The city's middle class is exploding and owning a car has suddenly become an attainable dream. One thousand new private cars are added to Beijing streets every day. Meanwhile, the 'grandparent' generation goes on as if little has changed, hanging out and chatting in the *hutong* (alleyways) or roaming the city parks, many still in their traditional Mao suits.

Despite all the social change, family remains the most important social unit in Chinese society; younger generations depend on older generations for wisdom and guidance, and older generations depend on the young for subsistence and care. China's One-Child Policy, instituted by Mao to avoid over-population, has changed the shape of families, creating a 4-2-1 balance (four grandparents, two parents and one child).

However, there are ongoing discussions about relaxing the one-child law in certain circumstances, such as allowing urban couples, who themselves are both only children, a permit for a second child.

The dominant beliefs in Beijing are Confucianism, Taoism and Buddhism. Buddhism and Taoism give reverence to gods and goddesses who preside over earth and the afterlife. Confucianism is more of a philosophy than a religion, dealing with the affairs of life but not of death. Confucianism defines codes of conduct and a patriarchal pattern of obedience; respect flows upwards from child to adult, woman to man and subject to ruler. Not surprisingly, it was adopted by the state for two millennia.

ARTS
MUSIC

Many Chinese folk songs can be traced back several hundred years and traditional musical concerts are still popular in Beijing. Performances feature the *sheng* (reed flute), the *erhu* (two-stringed fiddle), the *huqin* (two-stringed viola), the moon-shaped *yueqin* (four-stringed guitar), the *guzheng* (zither), the *pipa* (lute) and the ceremonial *suon* (trumpet). These instruments are also the musical stars of Chinese opera.

Beijing also has a thriving contemporary music scene. Musician (and Beijinger) Cui Jian (b 1961) kick-started the capital's rock scene in the late 1980s and laid the groundwork for punk bands like Underground Baby and metal groups like Tang Dynasty. These days, musicians from all over the country settle in the capital, attracted by its reputation as China's rock-music mecca. Punk and heavy metal remain inexplicably popular at many local clubs, though local musicians experimenting with hip-hop and pop music are making inroads. In the meantime, the bands with the buzz include the punk-styled group Subs and the manic live shows of grunge trio Cold Blooded Animal (Lengxue Dongwu).

STRINGS ATTACHED

Guanxi, or 'connections', string together much of Chinese society; you're either in the loop or you're not. It's the old practice of 'you scratch my back and I'll scratch yours'. In business it's referred to as 'going through the back door' and it can lead to anything from tickets on an oversold train to a job you have no qualifications for. When you meet Chinese people, the conversation may turn to what you've got to offer and how they can help you – they're throwing you the *guanxi* line.

BACKGROUND

PAINTING

A traditional Chinese painting may be achieved following much thought and total conception of the piece in the artist's mind beforehand. The brush line, which varies in thickness and tone, is the important feature; shading is regarded as a foreign technique and colour plays only a minor symbolic and decorative role. Figure painting dominated the scene from the Han dynasty (206 BC–AD 220) until Taoist painters began landscape painting in the 4th and 5th centuries.

It wasn't until the 20th century that there was any real departure from tradition. In the early days of communism, artistic talent was used to glorify the revolution. These days you'll find a flourishing avant-garde art scene in Beijing, with young artists gaining critical acclaim worldwide. For more on the contemporary art scene at Factory 798, see p16. For other hot galleries, see p130.

LITERATURE

Over time, Beijing has both produced and attracted well-known authors. Lao She, a novelist of the early 20th century, penned numerous novels in the capital; see p142. Other important 20th-century writers who resided in Beijing include Lu Xun, Mao Dun and Guo Moruo.

When the communists came to power, writing became a hazardous occupation and many writers did not survive. These days the situation has improved somewhat; writers continue to skirt around politically taboo issues but do explore social realities including alienation and confusion as tradition gives way to capitalism. Author Zhang Jie has been labelled China's first feminist writer for her internationally acclaimed *Love Must Not Be Forgotten*. More recently, Chun Shu's novel *Beijing Doll* and Annie Wang's *The People's Republic of Desire* have caused controversy for their discussion of sexuality in modern Beijing.

GOVERNMENT & POLITICS

Communist by name if not entirely by nature, China's central government has its quarters in Beijing, although precious little is known about its inner workings.

The current president is Hu Jintao (b 1942), a former engineer (and ballroom dancing aficionado) from Jiangsu province. Wen Jiabao (b 1942) is the Chinese premier and was born in Tianjin, which neighbours Beijing.

Political competition is not tolerated in China and political debate in public has long been a dangerous and therefore infrequent activity. Beijing is an independent municipality within Hubei province, with its own mayor; however, like many national capitals, the municipality is directly under the control of the central government.

ECONOMY

China is the fourth-largest economy in the world (after the United States, Japan and Germany), but if its current annual economic growth of over 10% per year continues, it may well be the world's largest economy within our lifetime.

While some predict the Chinese economy will be the world's largest by 2020, it's difficult to know what the true picture is: mass corruption leads to catastrophically inaccurate statistics and also sends around 13% to 17% of the GDP toward unlawful ends.

While the number of shops and shoppers in Beijing make the economic picture look shiny and bright, unemployment is on the rise and you will encounter the urban poor as well as the rural poor who have come to the city in an attempt to find work.

Increasingly, state-owned enterprises are being bought out or shut down; many laid-off workers feel the government has abandoned them to the market economy, and social unrest is beginning to rumble. In an attempt to stimulate the economy, the government is pouring money into public-works projects and welcoming foreign investment.

In Beijing, much of the economic boom is thanks to these public-works projects as well as state investment. The city, near neither coast nor inland waterway, is hampered by its geographic location in some respects and has completely missed out on the trade-fuelled economy enjoyed by rival Shanghai.

ENVIRONMENT

Beijing's air pollution is the stuff of legend and can get so bad, Beijingers can go weeks without seeing the sky. Beijing's air quality often measures five times the safety levels recommended by the World Health Organization. Only since Beijing was awarded the 2008 Summer Olympics has the government tackled the problem in a serious way. Polluting factories have been shut down (or, more often than not, just relocated outside

Beijing). Though government proclamations are regularly issued on the environment, they haven't had much impact on the day-to-day smog and pollution levels. Some Olympic teams have started to get worried and are developing back-up plans. While short-distance athletes aren't expected to experience severe problems, many teams are planning to keep their endurance athletes away from Beijing (in places like Japan) until the day before their events to minimise the impact pollution may have on their athletic performance.

In the meantime, the government has been experimenting with vehicle bans in downtown Beijing, allowing only odd or even-numbered license plates into the city at particular times. Though this keeps an estimated 1.5 million vehicles off the road each day it's enforced, it's had a negligible impact on overall air quality. Olympic officials have already floated the idea of postponing some endurance events if the pollution is not brought under control.

Elsewhere, Chinese scientists are getting in on the action and are experimenting with rockets that could be shot into the sky to clear the air of any storm or rain clouds that menace the Games.

Similar methods are already being used to shoot rain-inducing chemicals into the clouds to quench Beijing's parched atmosphere. As the area's population mushrooms, water tables are dropping and reservoirs are being drawn dry faster than they can be replenished. The city faces the real possibility of a future water shortage and many believe this will be the next big environmental issue after the Games have packed up and gone home.

FURTHER READING

In comparison to all the China-related books published each year, English-language Beijing-specific titles have always been thin on the ground. This is slowing changing, however, and there are several books worth looking over before you take your trip.

In addition to the books mentioned in the Literature section (p140), several other titles will help you unravel the sights and sounds of Beijing's past and present. Lao She's *Rickshaw Boy* (1936) is a window into the living conditions of rickshaw drivers in the early 20th century. *Twilight in the Forbidden City* (1934) by Reginald F Johnston describes the author's days tutoring the last emperor of China. *The Siege at Peking* (1959) by Peter Fleming is an excellent account of the Boxer Rebellion in Beijing, while *The Tiananmen Papers*, compiled by Zhang Liang (2002), blows away the official smokescreen hanging over 4 June 1989.

Foreign Babes in Beijing: Behind the Scenes of a New China (2005) by American Rachel DeWoskin is a light-hearted memoir of the author's time working on a Chinese soap opera in the capital. *Beijing: From Imperial Capital to Olympic City* (2007) is an excellent overview of the city's history by Lillian M Li, Alison Dray-Novey and Haili Kong. And Ma Jian's *Red Dust*, though a memoir of his travels throughout China, gives a fascinating peek into the lives of Beijing's artistic community in the 1980s.

FILMS

Some of the most acclaimed films about modern Beijing include Wang Xiaoshuai's *Beijing Bicycle*, a sometimes violent film about a courier on the trail of his stolen bike; Jia Zhangke's *The World* (2005), set in Beijing's kitchy 'World Park' theme-park; and Yuan Zhang's *Bastards* (1993), a documentary exploring Beijing's rock scene featuring Cui Jian.

Ning Ying has done several films in the last decade exploring regular people's lives in Beijing. Her latest, *Perpetual Motion* (2005), chronicles an evening in the life of four Beijing women who gather for some hefty talk on the eve of Chinese New Year.

There are several excellent feature films about historical Beijing. Bernardo Bertolucci's *The Last Emperor* (1987) won a truckload of Oscars and chronicles the demise of China's last dynasty. Chen Kaige's *Farewell My Concubine* (1993) is a fascinating and beautifully shot film set in the world of Peking opera.

DIRECTORY
TRANSPORT
ARRIVAL & DEPARTURE

International travellers arrive and depart from Beijing's Capital International Airport. Travellers going to or coming from Hong Kong or Shanghai have air and rail options.

AIR

Beijing's **Capital International Airport** (北京首都国际机场; http://en.bcia .com.cn) is about 25km northeast of the city centre. Most arrivals and departures will be at Terminal 2 until June 2008. Terminal 3 is under construction and will be opened in time for the 2008 Olympic Games, serving both international and domestic flights. A subway/light rail link from Capital International Airport to Dongzhimen in Beijing is under construction, also due for completion for the Games. Passengers will be able to transfer to the subway system from Dongzhimen Station.

Departure taxes are included in plane ticket prices.

TRAIN

A daily train service runs to and from Hong Kong (Y558, 26 hours) with trains arriving and departing from **Beijing West Train Station** (北京西 站; ☎ 5182 6273) in Fengtai. Several fast ('Z') trains also run daily to and from Shanghai (Y466 to Y486, 11½ hours). Most non-Chinese speakers prefer to pay a small surcharge and buy train tickets through their accommodation. Buying tickets at Beijing's train stations can be an overwhelming and chaotic experience. Tickets can also be bought online at www.chinatripadvisor .com and www.china-train-ticket .com if you're in China.

VISA

Visas are required for everyone visiting mainland China. A standard

---

CLIMATE CHANGE & TRAVEL

Travel – especially air travel – is a significant contributor to global climate change. At Lonely Planet, we believe that all who travel have a responsibility to limit their personal impact. As a result, we have teamed with Rough Guides and other concerned industry partners to support Climate Care, which allows people to offset the greenhouse gases they are responsible for with contributions to energy-saving projects and other climate-friendly initiatives in the developing world. Lonely Planet offsets all staff and author travel.

For more information, turn to the responsible-travel pages on www.lonelyplanet .com. For details on offsetting your carbon emissions and a carbon calculator, go to www .climatecare.org.

TAXIS FROM THE AIRPORT

A long-running and well-established illegal taxi ring operates inside the arrivals hall of Terminal 2. One man acts as a pimp for drivers outside and lures exhausted travellers to fake cabs that charge Y300 (or more) for rides into town. Don't fall for this – make sure you line up at the taxi stand outside.

The majority of Beijing taxi drivers are honest, but travellers have occasionally reported problems on the run from the airport into town. Usually, this involves the driver not turning on the meter and charging inflated bills. Airport authorities have started cracking down. Clerks now staff the airport taxi stand writing down the taxi number and your destination on a 'passenger direct card' so you can follow up if you think there's been any funny business.

30-day, single-entry visa is readily available from Chinese embassies and consulates and usually takes three to five working days.

GETTING AROUND

Beijing is a pain to get around. Distances are huge, the public transportation network is desperately overcrowded and heavy traffic often slows buses and taxis to a complete standstill during the day. The subway is the most reliable way to get around, though the underdeveloped system only gets you to a handful of the city's main sights. Taxis are cheap, plentiful and the most convenient way to get around Beijing but are best avoided between 8am and 10am and between 5pm and 7pm, when travel times can as much as quadruple. Combining a subway and taxi ride is generally the best way to get around. Thanks to the Olympic Games, authorities are modernising Beijing's infrastructure mess, so expect to see marked improvement from 2008 on. New subway lines are slated to open regularly until at least 2015.

SUBWAY

Beijing's subway lines start running between 5am and 6am and close between 10.30pm and 11pm. Purchase your ticket (Y2) inside the stations. For more information, and to check which new subway lines may have opened, check www.bjsubway.com/ens/index.html. In this book, the nearest subway station is noted after the subway icon (🚇) in each listing.

TAXI

The flag-fall and first 3km is Y10. It's Y2 for each kilometre after

GETTING TO & FROM TERMINAL 2

	Taxi	Airport bus	Subway (approx opening June 2008)
Pick-up point	outside Exit 5 at arrivals	outside Exit 11 at arrivals	follow signs in terminals
Drop-off points	anywhere	Line A: Dongzhimen, Beijing Railway Station; Line B: Youyi Hotel (Renmin University of China), Beijing TV Station; Line C: Yuyang Hotel, Chaoyangmen, North Wangfujing (Dongsi Art Museum)	last stop Dongzhimen Subway Station
Duration	to Tiananmen Sq 60min (light traffic)	average 60-90min to last stop	15-20min (light traffic)
Cost	to Tiananmen Sq Y90-100 (light traffic)	Y16	TBC
Other	Y15 airport expressway toll	Line A runs 8am-last flight; Lines B & C 8am-10.30pm	TBC
Contact	flag down on street	http://en.bcia.com.cn/harbor-guide/iarrive.shtml	www.bjsubway.com/ens/index.html

that. Between 11pm and 6am there is a 20% surcharge added to the flag-fall metered fare. Taxi drivers do not speak English so have your destination written down in characters or circled on a Chinese-language map. At the end of the trip, pay what's on the meter plus any expressway tolls the driver has ponied up for. Once the taxi ride is underway, the driver should turn on the meter. If he or she doesn't, ask them to turn it on (da biao; 打表). Ask for the receipt (fapiao; 发票) when your trip is over. The driver's ID number will be on it so you'll be able to track them down if you've left something in the car or need to make a complaint.

You can also hire taxis for the day but must negotiate the rate with the driver depending on where you want to go – Y400 is the minimum rate.

BUS

Overcrowded and frustratingly slow, Beijing's city buses are time-sappers for those on short visits and problematic for non-Chinese speakers. However, two **'Tourism' bus stations** (☎ 24hr info line 8353 1111) offer direct services to some far-flung sights. Buses bring you to and from the destinations but are not part of guided tours – you explore the sights on your own.

The **Tourism Bus Station** (Map p87, D6; Qianmen Xidajie), west off Tiananmen Square, is well-run and easy to navigate. Buses to Badaling Great Wall (Y90, see p108) leave when full between 7.30am and11.30am. It takes about 60 minutes to reach the wall (though rush-hour traffic can easily double that). You'll have around two hours to visit.

The Badaling Great Wall and Ming Tombs bus (Y160) is another popular option. Buses leave from the Tourism Bus Station off Tiananmen Sq when full between 6.30am and 10.30am. This is a full-day trip visiting both sights.

Nearby, the **Tourism Bus Station** (Map p87, C6; Xuanwumen Xidajie), near the South Cathedral, is less user-friendly (tickets are only sold between 6.30am and 7.50am and buses are cancelled if fewer than 15 people show up) but it has services to Simatai Great Wall (p109) for Y95 at 8.30am on Saturday and Sunday, with a four-hour visit at the wall. Services also run to Tanzhe Temple (p112) for Y90, departing 8.30am Sunday. This is a full-day trip often coupled with stops at such places as a stalagmite cave and/or a dingy amusement park.

BICYCLE

For information on cycling around the capital, see p129.

BOAT

Boats (adult/child Y40/25) travel from Xicheng district to the Summer Palace (p83) along Beijing's Qing-era canal network. They run hourly 10am to 4pm from May to October. You can leave from the dock at the zoo (Map p81, B6) or the dock behind the nearby Beijing Exhibition Centre (Map p87, A2).

PRACTICALITIES
BUSINESS HOURS

Stores, offices and banks are generally open Monday to Friday from 9am until 5pm or 6pm. Offices and banks outside the downtown core and main tourist drags also sometimes close for an hour or two at lunch time. Malls and department stores are generally open from 10am to 9pm. Restaurants are open 11am to 2pm and 5.30pm to 10pm. Most sights are open daily, including public holidays, though some of the bigger museums are closed on Monday.

INFORMATION & ORGANISATIONS

The **Chinese Culture Club** (Map pp54-5, F1; ☎ 6432 934; www.chinesecultureclub .org; 29 Liangmaqiao Lu, Anjialou, 亮马桥路29号安家搂) is geared to expats but open to everyone and offers excellent English-language tours, lectures and courses.

RECOMMENDED MODES OF TRANSPORT

	Lama Temple	Sanlitun Lu	Panjiayuan Antique Market
Lama Temple	n/a	taxi 20min	subway to Guomao 15min + taxi 15min
Sanlitun Lu	taxi 20min	n/a	taxi to Dongsishitiao 10min + subway to Guomao 10min + taxi 15min
Panjiayuan Antique Market	taxi to Guomao 15min + subway to Yonghegong-Lama Temple 15min	taxi to Guomao 15min + subway to Dongsishitiao 10min + taxi 10min	n/a
Temple of Heaven	subway to Yonghegong-Lama Temple 23min	subway to Dongsishitiao 20min + taxi 10min	taxi 20min
Niujie Mosque	taxi to Changchunjie 10min + subway to Yonghegong-Lama Temple 18min	taxi to Changchunjie 10min + subway to Dongsishitiao 17min + taxi 10min	taxi 35min
Houhai Lake	subway to Yonghegong-Lama Temple 4min	subway to Dongsishitiao 9min + taxi 10min	subway to Guomao 18min + taxi 15min
Summer Palace	taxi to Wudaokou 15min + subway to Yonghegong-Lama Temple 20min	taxi to Wudaokou 15min + subway to Donsishitiao 26min + taxi 10min	taxi to Wudaokou 15min + subway to Guomao 38min + taxi 15min

DISCOUNTS

Children under a certain height (specified at each site) often get in free or for half price. If you can produce a student ID or an **ISIC card** (www.isiccard.com), you may get a discount rate, though some sights offer discount student rates only to those studying at Chinese universities. For museum-pass info see the boxed text on p42.

ELECTRICITY

Electricity is 220V, 50 Hz. Beijing plugs vary, so you'll see up to four different sorts in some older hotel rooms. If you plan to use/recharge electronic devices from home, bring a good plug-adapter kit.

EMERGENCIES

Compared to cities of similar size, Beijing is one of the safest urban

	Temple of Heaven	Niujie Mosque	Houhai Lake	Summer Palace
	subway to Tiantandongmen 23min	subway to Changchunjie 18min + taxi 10min	subway to Gulou Dajie 4min	subway to Wudaokou 20min + taxi 15min
	taxi to Dongsishitiao 10min + subway to Tiantandongmen 20min	taxi to Dongsishitiao 10min + subway to Changchunjie 17min + taxi 10min	taxi to Dongsishitiao 10min + subway to Gulou Dajie 9min	taxi to Dongsishitiao 10min + subway to Wudaokou 26min + taxi 15min
	taxi 20min	taxi 35min	taxi to Guomao 15min + subway to Gulou Dajie 18min	taxi to Guomao 15min + subway to Wudaokou 38min + taxi 15min
	n/a	taxi 20min	subway to Gulou Dajie 23min	subway to Wudaokou 36min + taxi 15min
	taxi 20min	n/a	taxi to Changchunjie 10min + subway to Gulou Dajie 14min	taxi to Changchunjie 10min + subway to Wudaokou 18min + taxi 15min
	subway to Tiantandongmen 23min	subway to Changchunjie 14min + taxi 10min	n/a	subway to Wudaokou 16min + taxi 15min
	taxi to Wudaokou 15min + subway to Tiantandongmen 36min	taxi to Wudaokou 15min + subway to Changchunjie 18min + taxi 10min	taxi to Wudaokou 15min + subway to Golou Dajie 16min	n/a

centres in the world. Serious or violent crimes involving visitors are rare. All that most travellers need to be on guard against is pick-pocketing (which is rampant) and certain scams targeting foreigners, such as the taxi scam (see p145), counterfeit money (see p153) and other confidence tricks (see p46).

Ambulance ☎ 120
Fire ☎ 119
Police ☎ 110

Public Security Bureau (foreigners' section) ☎ 8402 0101

HOLIDAYS

New Year's Day 1 January
Spring Festival (Chinese New Year) Generally held in January or February; 7 February 2008, 26 January 2009, 14 February 2010 (see p26)
International Women's Day 8 March
International Labour Day 1 May
Youth Day 4 May
International Children's Day 1 June

Birthday of the Chinese Communist Party 1 July
Anniversary of the founding of the People's Liberation Army (PLA) 1 August
National Day 1 October

INTERNET

Beijing's internet cafés (*wangba*, 网吧) are often squirreled away down *hutong* (alleyways) or in the basements or upper floors of buildings on side streets, so keep your eyes peeled for the Chinese characters. Expect to pay between Y2 and Y5 per hour. Connections can be frustratingly slow, especially for heavily used sites like Hotmail. Internet access is readily available at hostels (usually around Y10 per hour) and hotel business centres. Rates at midrange Chinese hotels sometimes start at Y30 per hour, while those at foreign-owned top-end accommodation can run to Y180 per hour. Government censors sometimes block foreign websites (BBC News is a perennial favourite) containing content critical of China or the Communist Party.

Wi-fi (wireless internet; *gaobaozhen*, 高保真) zones are increasingly common in Beijing, especially in expat-oriented restaurants and cafés like Bookworm (p62). Check www.chinapulse.com for a complete list of wi-fi hotspots.

INTERNET RESOURCES

In addition to www.lonelyplanet.com, interesting China-related websites include www.hanzismatter.com and www.zhongwen.com for info on the Chinese language. Sites touching on life and culture in China include www.danwei.org and www.rockinchina.com.

LANGUAGE

The official language of the People's Republic of China is Putonghua, based on (but not identical to) the Beijing Mandarin dialect.

Written Chinese script is based on ancient pictograph characters that have been simplified over time; while over 56,000 characters have been verified, it is commonly held that a well-educated Chinese person knows and uses between 6000 and 8000 characters. Pinyin has been developed as a Romanisation of Mandarin using English letters, but many Beijingers cannot read it.

A growing number of Beijingers speak some English; in tourist hotels and restaurants and at major sights you'll get along OK without Mandarin. But if you venture into shops, neighbourhoods or conversations that are off the tourist track, you may find yourself lost for words. Names and addresses are provided in Chinese characters throughout this book to use when you're taking taxis. It's also useful to have the concierge of your hotel write down your address in Chinese before you go anywhere.

For a user-friendly guide, with pronunciation tips and a phrase list (including script that you can simply show to people rather than speak), get a copy of Lonely Planet's *Mandarin* phrasebook.

BASICS

See also the Quick Reference section on the inside front cover.

Hello.
Nǐ hǎo. 你好。
Goodbye.
Zàijiàn. 再见。
Please.
Qǐng. 请。
Thank you.
Xièxie. 谢谢。
Yes.
Shìde. 是的。
No. (don't have)
Méi yǒu. 没有。
No. (not so)
Bùshì. 不是。
Do you speak English?
Nǐ huì shuō Yīngyǔ ma? 你会说英语吗？
Do you understand?
Dǒng ma? 懂吗？
I understand.
Wǒ tīngdedǒng. 我听得懂。
Could you please ...?
Nǐ néng bunéng ...? 你能不能…？
repeat that
chóngfù 重复

speak more slowly
shuō màn diǎnr 说慢点儿
write it down
xiě xiàlái 写下来

EATING & DRINKING

I don't want MSG.
Wǒ bù yào wèijīng. 我不要味精。
I'm vegetarian.
Wǒ chī sù. 我吃素。
Not too spicy.
Bùyào tàilà. 不要太辣。
Let's eat!
Chī fàn! 吃饭！
Cheers!
Gānbēi! 干杯！
menu
càidān 菜单
bill (cheque)
mǎi dān/jiézhàng 买单/结帐

GOING OUT

What's on ...?
... yǒu shénme yúlè huódòng? …有什么娱乐活动？
this weekend
zhège zhōumò 这个周末
today
jīntiān 今天
tonight
jīntiān wǎnshang 今天晚上
Where are the ...?
... zài nǎr? …在哪儿？
clubs
jùlèbù 俱乐部
gay venues
tóngxìngliàn chǎngsuǒ 同性恋场所
places to eat
chīfàn de dìfang 吃饭的地方
pubs
jiǔbā 酒吧

INTERNET

Is there a local internet café?
Běndì yǒu wǎngbā ma?
本地有网吧吗？

Where can I get online?
Wǒ zài nǎr kěyǐ shàngwǎng?
我在哪儿可以上网？

TRANSPORT

Please use the meter.
Qǐng dǎ biǎo.　　请打表。

How much (is it) to ...?
Qù ... dūoshǎo qián?　去…多少钱？

EMERGENCIES

It's an emergency!
Zhèshì jǐnjí qíngkuàng!
这是紧急情况！

Could you help me, please?
Nǐ néng bunéng bāng wǒ ge máng?
你能不能帮我个忙？

Call the police/a doctor/an ambulance!
Qǐng jiào jǐngchá/yīshēng/jiùhùchē!
请叫警察/医生/救护车！

Where's the police station?
Pàichūsuǒ zài nǎr?
派出所在哪儿？

NUMBERS

1	*yī/yāo*	一/幺
2	*èr/liǎng*	二/两
3	*sān*	三
4	*sì*	四
5	*wǔ*	五
6	*liù*	六
7	*qī*	七
8	*bā*	八
9	*jiǔ*	九
10	*shí*	十
20	*èrshí*	二十
30	*sānshí*	三十
40	*sìshí*	四十
50	*wǔshí*	五十
60	*liùshí*	六十
70	*qīshí*	七十
80	*bāshí*	八十
90	*jiǔshí*	九十
100	*yìbǎi*	一百
1000	*yìqiān*	一千

DAYS

Monday	*xīngqīyī*	星期一
Tuesday	*xīngqī'èr*	星期二
Wednesday	*xīngqīsān*	星期三
Thursday	*xīngqīsì*	星期四
Friday	*xīngqīwǔ*	星期五
Saturday	*xīngqīliù*	星期六
Sunday	*xīngqītiān*	星期天

....

MONEY

COSTS

Whether you're a big-spender, counting your pennies or somewhere in between, you'll be able to find your niche in Beijing. If you stay at cheap hostels, eat at small neighbourhood restaurants and don't buy anything, you can get by on Y250 per day. At the top end of things, the sky is the limit with increasing numbers of swish restaurants, luxury stores and deluxe hotel rooms at Y2000 or more. Beijing's modernisation is driving up the prices, especially of midrange accommodation. See the Quick Reference section on the inside front cover for exchange rates.

COUNTERFEIT MONEY

Counterfeit money is rampant in Beijing so expect heavy inspection of your paper money before it is accepted. Foreigners are the prime targets for fake bills – especially with 50 and 100 yuan notes. To check the money yourself, turn the bill Mao-side up and stroke the bottom right hand corner. The design should feel raised. Next, hold it to the light: a ghostly Mao should be hovering on the left-hand side. Don't be shy about handing suspicious money back. Vendors will usually hand you a different bill without a fuss.

CURRENCY

Chinese currency is called Renminbi (RMB) or 'people's money'. Its basic unit is the yuan (Y), called *kua'* or *kuaiqian* in spoken Chinese. The yuan is divided into 10 jiao (referred to as *mao* in spoken Chinese). The jiao is divided into 10 fen. These days, fen are worth next to nothing and are disappearing from use.

Paper notes are issued in denominations of one, two, five, 10, 20, 50 and 100 yuan; one, two and five jiao; and one, two and five fen. Coins are in denominations of one yuan; one, two and five jiao; and one, two and five fen.

TRAVELLERS CHEQUES

Travellers cheques issued by leading banks and issuing agencies like Citibank, American Express or Visa can be cashed in Beijing at the Bank of China, exchange desks at the airport and, if you are a guest, at large upscale tourist hotels. If you're doing any day trips, cash cheques beforehand; banks

in Beijing's far-flung regions and countryside often don't handle travellers cheques.

CREDIT CARDS

Most four- and five-star hotels, fancy restaurants and major department stores accept credit cards. If you use your credit card for a cash advance at the Bank of China or CITIC Bank, you'll pay a steep 4% commission.

ATMS

ATMs accepting foreign bank and credit cards are becoming common in Beijing's main shopping areas like Wangfujing Dajie (Map pp40–1, C6) as well as central Bank of China branches. ATMs outside of these areas often take only Chinese cards so check for the GlobalAccess, Cirrus, Interlink, Plus or Star symbols before you start.

CHANGING MONEY

Foreign currency can be exchanged at the Bank of China,

exchange desks at the airport, and, if you're a guest, at top-end and some upper midrange hotels. Banks give the official rate, as do most hotels. Hold on to your exchange receipts. You may be asked for them if you want to exchange RMB back to foreign currency (to prove you didn't get the money off the black market).

NEWSPAPERS & MAGAZINES

Beijing has a whopping number of free English-language entertainment magazines. *That's Beijing* (www.thatsbj.com) is the biggest and most comprehensive. Other good ones are *Time Out Beijing*, *City Weekend* (www.cityweekend .com.cn) and *Beijing This Month* (www.btmbeijing.com). The pro-government, English-language *China Daily* (www.chinadaily.com .cn) is dismal on the news front but occasionally has worthwhile cultural and travel profiles.

ORGANISED TOURS

For tours, the **China Culture Club** (Map pp54-5, F1; ☎ 6432 934; www.chineseculture club.org; 29 Liangmaqiao Lu, Anjialou, 亮马 桥路29号安家楼) offers the best quality and variety of English-language tours in town covering things like architecture, *hutong* or the Forbidden City. Check the website for schedules.

If the Back Lakes of Xicheng interest you, you may like **River Romance** (好梦江南; ☎ 6612 5717; www.haomengjiangnan.com), which takes you for an hour-long bob on Qianhai Lake (Y300/200 with /without traditional music).

PHOTOGRAPHY & VIDEO

Film and digital photo equipment and accessories are available all over Beijing and often in stalls near major tourist sights. The Kodak Express (Map pp40–1, B8) branch just off Tiananmen Square sells film and memory cards and burns CDs for Y15.

TELEPHONE

International and domestic calls are easily made from your hotel room or public phones. Local calls from hotel rooms are often free (check first) but international phone calls are expensive and it's better to use a phonecard (see opposite). Local calls can also easily be made from public phones (usually bright red or orange) at newspaper stands and hole-in-the-wall shops. You pay the owner when you're done.

To call a Beijing number from abroad, dial the international access code (00 in the UK, 011 in the USA), dial the country code for China (86) and then the area code for Beijing (010), dropping the first zero, and then dial the local number. For telephone calls within the same city, drop the area code. If calling internationally from Beijing or from China, drop the first zero of the area or city code after dialling the international access code and then dial the number you wish to call.

MOBILE PHONES

If your cell phone from home uses a SIM card, it may work in China once you've purchased a Beijing SIM card (Y60 to Y100). However, ask your network provider at home whether you need to have the phone unlocked before you leave. Credit-charging cards (*chongzhi ka*, 充值卡; Y50 and Y100) are sold at most kiosks and convenience stores. You can buy SIM cards from China Mobile or China Unicom shops; they're located seemingly on every street corner. The China Mobile network has the best China-wide coverage.

PHONECARDS

IP (internet phone) cards (*IP ka*, IP 卡) are best for making international calls and come in various denominations. Most cards either have English instructions on them or give an English-language service number to call. IC (integrated circuit; *IC ka*, IC 卡) cards are for domestic calls; they can be used at most public phones. IP and IC cards are sold in kiosks, hole-in-the-wall shops, China Telecom offices and most hotel business centres.

COUNTRY & CITY CODES

Australia ☎ 61
Canada ☎ 1
France ☎ 33
New Zealand ☎ 64
UK ☎ 44
USA ☎ 1

Beijing ☎ 010
Hong Kong ☎ 852
Shanghai ☎ 021

TIPPING

Hotel porters in upscale hotels will expect something but tipping is not otherwise customary in Beijing. Waiters and taxi drivers will be confused and offended if you leave money behind (and often run after you to give it back). Despite this, many foreigners have insisted on throwing their money around and, in order to accommodate them, many midrange and upscale restaurants owners have added a 10-15% 'service charge' to final bills to relieve them of their money formally, though this is often kept by the restaurant and not distributed among the servers. Many restaurants and cafés that are foreign-oriented also put out tipping jars to which you can contribute.

TOURIST INFORMATION

Though many things in Beijing are being successfully modernised, tour services for foreigners aren't yet among them. English skills in most city and government tourism offices are still nonexistent and foreigners' tour and information needs often leave tour and tourism staff completely bewildered. There's a **Beijing Tourism Hotline** (☎ 6513 0828; ⏱ 24hr) with English-speaking operators available (press '1' after dialling the number) to answer questions and hear complaints but your best source of travel info is usually at your accommodation or travel-oriented expat hangouts like Passby Bar (p50). See also Organised Tours (p154).

TRAVELLERS WITH DISABILITIES

Beijing is a challenge for anyone with mobility disabilities. There are no elevators and in the subway stations if there is an escalator, it is usually broken or only going up. Though most new buildings and some major sights are being made more 'handi-capped accessible' this is often in name only. Ramps may be added in some places and not in others, toilets marked wheelchair accessible are often missing things like hand-rails or aren't wide enough to accommodate standard chair dimensions. Sidewalks are over-crowded and in poor condition and curbs prevent wheelchair access. Those with sight, hearing or walking disabilities must also be extremely cautious of the traffic, which does not yield to pedestrians. It's best to contact your local disability association for advice before leaving.

>INDEX

See also separate subindexes for See (166), Shop (p167), Eat (p167), Drink (p168) and Play (p168).

000 map pages

INDEX

⊙ SEE

000 map pages